Copyright © Kath Lee 2014
All rights reserved
No part of this book may be reproduced, stored in a retrieval system or transmitted in any form without prior permission of the author.

1st Printing

Available on most e-devices and similar

ISBN 13: 978-1494758165
ISBN 10: 1494758164

Leximo Publishing
Kathle1.wix.com/kathlee

DYING FOR ANSWERS

BY

KATH LEE

THE WRITER

Kath trained as a secretary and worked in industry before leaving to have her two children. When they were small she returned to full time education. She graduated from Coventry University and then went on to Warwick University
where she obtained a Masters and a social work qualification. She spent many years working in social work and related professions. She has two grown up children and two grand-daughters.
She recently retired and now has the time to concentrate on her writing. This is Kath's second book. She recently published a novel Aspiration Perspiration Desperation inspired by her career in social work.

ACKNOWLEDGEMENTS

There are so many people who deserve heartfelt thanks for helping me along the road to completing this book but I would especially like to express my gratitude to the following people:

The late Ron Watkins, without whose advice the journey might never have begun.
My dear friends who "travelled" with me, the late Ann Coleman, Mary and the late Pete Reilly, Gill Bayton and Veronica Moore, all of whom are very special people without whose help I may have fallen by the wayside.

Thanks to Colin's beloved daughter, Sarah Robinson, who travelled the long sad road with me.

And finally my own dear family who offered enormous support and who picked me up when I fell – Kate who was my rock, Matt, John, Brian and Val who were always there for me, and Andrew who was a pillar of strength and an inspiration.

Thanks to Edwina and Veronica for reading the initial manuscript and making some invaluable suggestions.

A very special thank you, to Margaret Fairhurst for her diligent proof-reading and editing skills.

You are all stars and I would like to say "thank you" from the bottom of my heart.

DEDICATION

Colin was a very special man and the world is a much poorer place without him in it.

He had a great love and respect for people and the ability to make everyone feel a little bit special. He was selfless, sensitive and caring but strong and capable. He possessed Irish charm by the bucketful. He was bossy at times but always so understanding. He had a great sense of fun and he brought laughter into all our lives. He possessed a sense of adventure and lived his life to the full. He was the eternal optimist and an easy man to love. He was a cherished and adored partner, father, grandfather and friend.

He gave me many gifts and the most precious of these was his love. I feel that I was indeed fortunate to have shared my life with such an amazing man who will live in my heart forever. I would not have wanted to miss a single moment of it!

After all the sadness, I can now think of Colin and smile as I recall the incredible experiences we shared. He can still make me laugh when I remember the funny times. That is how he would wish it to be. He will be loved and adored forever and this book is dedicated to him and the wonderful memories he has left behind.

PREFACE

My partner Colin died in January 2002 after being admitted to hospital for routine investigations. His death was shocking and at the subsequent inquest, the Coroner expressed the view that his care fell far short of the standard that should have been expected. In spite of this, the hospital Trust behaved in what I consider to be an unacceptable manner and it took three years to get the apology he deserved. When an apology was eventually issued it was wheeled out with the old adage, **"lessons have been learned"**.

This phrase is a perennial favourite of those defending the indefensible within the NHS and I have heard it so many times since Colin died. If only it were true!

Eleven years on, I question what lessons have **really** been learned. On a daily basis reports appear in the Media of yet another pointless death at the hands of the Hospital Trusts and the nation witnesses scandals such as those at Stafford Hospital whilst eleven other NHS Trusts are placed into special measures.

When Colin died, I was of the opinion that he was one of the few unlucky ones who had the misfortune to be in hospital at Christmas time (a notoriously risky time for surgery) and that he had somehow ended up with the wrong doctor or treatment. In short, he was in the wrong place at the wrong time. I believed that he was the exception to the rule. Subsequent events have proved that he was just one of thousands who misplaced their trust in the NHS and became a statistic.

I believe that there are systemic failures within the NHS and a bullying culture which pervades it. This prevents staff from admitting their mistakes and I feel that in desperation families are forced to consult lawyers because it is the only way they can discover what happened and get truthful answers to the questions they have about the treatment received by their loved ones. This litigation is costing the NHS billions and making law firms very wealthy, when all that is needed is a culture of openness and transparency because the majority of people do not wish to go to litigation but feel it is the only choice open to them.

I also believe that there are some brilliant and caring individuals who work tirelessly in the system and who must be totally demoralised at the continued revelations of poor care and resultant deaths within the service.

Whilst there are thousands of professional and genuine people working conscientiously within the NHS, events following Colin's death convinced me that some staff have little integrity or compassion and just do not care enough for those placed in their care.

At the time of Colin's death, I felt I should write a book about our treatment at the hands of the NHS Trust so that others might learn and benefit from those experiences. However, I chose not to because I felt that I needed to try to move forward.

I now feel moved to write this book because I have come to realise that the nature of Colin's death was not a rare occurrence. I believe that few lessons have genuinely been learned in eleven years and I hope that reading my story might give someone the strength to fight for justice within the NHS and also how to go about it because this might drive the changes so sorely needed.

I have written this book because I fervently care about the NHS and the principals that lead to its creation and it is my view that if it is to survive, it must learn from what it got wrong in each hospital and ensure these lessons are disseminated across the service so that good practice is shared.

CONTENTS		PAGE
CHAPTER 1	THE BEGINNING	1
CHAPTER 2	THE MISDIAGNOSIS	7
CHAPTER 3	THE TRUE DIAGNOSIS	11
CHAPTER 4	LIFE AND DEATH IN THE INTENSIVE CARE UNIT	19
CHAPTER 5	SAYING GOODBYE	39
CHAPTER 6	WHERE TO BEGIN?	47
CHAPTER 7	THE ROCKY ROAD TO THE INQUEST	53
CHAPTER 8	THE INQUEST	67
CHAPTER 9	WHAT NOW?	77
CHAPTER 10	THE ROAD TO JUSTICE	89
CHAPTER 11	THE END OF THE ROAD	97
CHAPTER 12	AIRING THE ISSUES	103
CHAPTER 13	CONCLUSION	107

CHAPTER 1
THE BEGINNING

My beloved partner and soul mate Colin was admitted to hospital on the 17th December 2001 suffering from a minor abdominal complaint and he was discharged in a body bag on the 11th January 2002. So began a chain of events which would change my life forever.

We had just returned from holiday and it was me rather than him who was feeling ill because I had developed a chest infection whilst abroad. When I began to feel a little better Colin, who had retired from work two weeks earlier, told me he was taking me to the Jewellery Quarter in Birmingham to buy me a ring for Christmas. After much to-ing and fro-ing between jewellers, we chose a Victorian ruby and diamond band which we both loved for its simplicity. He was so excited that I had found a ring I loved and his blue Irish eyes sparkled as we had lunch in a local wine bar. It was such a lovely day and one which I will remember forever.

That evening we had arranged to take my mother out to dinner and we took her to a local pub. It was really busy with crowds enjoying their pre-Christmas celebrations and the atmosphere was very festive. When we got home, Colin said that the meal was lying heavily on his stomach. He always kept to a low fat diet and complained that he felt the meal was very fatty.

On the 13th December, Colin went for a walk and when he returned he complained of feeling constipated, a condition from which he had never suffered. He went to the local chemist who advised that he should take some senna tablets which he did. There was no improvement in his condition.
We had arranged an evening out with my brother and sister in law, Brian and Val. We arrived at the pub and in spite of his condition Colin was on fine form. We spent the evening having a meal and planning a forthcoming trip to the Far East. Colin was Irish and fortune had bestowed upon him all the attributes for which his race is famous, wit, charm, humour and fun. He was magic, always full of life and laughter and this evening was no exception. When he said he had kissed the Blarney Stone, we argued that he had eaten it!!! We all had an excellent evening, including Colin and at this point there was no indication that he was anything other than completely fit and well.

On the 14th December, Colin felt a little concerned that he remained constipated in spite of the senna and so he used the NHS website to determine what might be causing his symptoms. He told me that he felt there may be an obstruction and as it was Saturday there was little he could do, but he intended to visit the GP on Monday.

On Sunday Colin's daughter Sarah, and her children Kyle and Lauren, came from Derbyshire to visit for the day. Colin adored his grandchildren and loved their visits. He was a very hands-on grand-father. He would play kung-fu and play fighting rolling around on the floor with them. They would leap on him and climb all over him and he would be in heaven. I noticed that today he was not quite as exuberant as normal and he was protecting his stomach from the Kung fu blows. When Sarah and the children left he told me he was going to lie down for a little while because he felt extremely uncomfortable.

On the Monday morning Colin visited Dr Wallace, our GP. This was a very rare occurrence as he was extremely fit and healthy and the only times she ever saw him previously were for routine issues such as flu jabs or travel vaccinations. The doctor gave Colin some medication and said that if this did not relieve his constipation over-night then he would need to be admitted to hospital next morning.

It did not improve and on the 17th December we collected a letter from the GP and went to the admissions unit at Walsgrave Hospital, Coventry.

I still find it really difficult to come to terms with events that followed. I had assumed that once we got to hospital and put our faith in the professionals all would soon be well and we would be home celebrating Christmas and replicating the previous joyous ones we had shared.

Despite the fact that Colin was being admitted to hospital he was still on good form. As we drove to the hospital he joked about them having to send for Dyno-rod. He certainly was not unduly worried and he told me not to worry. We arrived at the hospital at about 9.30 am and waited for an hour before he was called from the waiting room. He went through all the admissions procedures and then I joined him. We eventually saw a doctor at 11.30 am and X-rays and blood tests were taken. We were then left all day without further communication and we had no idea what was wrong with Colin and we were given no information. I spoke to a nurse on several occasions in an attempt to elicit some information, any information! I was eventually told that they were waiting for a surgeon to speak to Colin. I just found it difficult to understand that staff found it so problematic to communicate with patients. When people are anxious and concerned it is so important that they are communicated with, even if it is just to explain why the doctor has not appeared yet. At least they know that they have not been forgotten!

At about 5.00 pm Brian and Val arrived in Admissions. They had come to the hospital because they were aware that Colin had gone in at 9.00 am and were worried because they had not heard from me. They brought drinks and sandwiches and decided to stay until the doctor arrived as they were concerned about Colin.

Between 5.30 - 6.00 pm two doctors arrived in Colin's cubicle. One of these was Dr. Emmanuel Agaba, a registrar but Colin was admitted under the care of Mr Daniel Higman, who was the Consultant responsible. He held up an X-ray which had been taken in the morning and was very friendly and smiled reassuringly. He and Colin shared a little banter and he then said he had diagnosed the problem. We were all shown the X-ray and he said that on Colin's right hand side there was a strangulated hernia and this was on the site of an old appendectomy scar Colin had had since early childhood and he said that this was obstructing the colon. He also pointed out what he said was a reducible hernia on the left hand side of Colin's abdomen but went on to say that this was nothing to worry about. Dr Agaba said that it was his intention to operate that night to repair the hernia and to straighten out the piece of bowel that had become twisted. He did not suggest that any further tests were necessary.

Both Colin and I were relieved but surprised at this diagnosis because we understood that strangulated hernias caused intense pain. Whilst Colin's abdomen was distended, bloated and uncomfortable, he was not experiencing severe pain.

Brian and Val went home relieved that it was nothing more serious and I stayed at the hospital with Colin until about 9.30 pm when he said that if I did not leave, he would have the staff throw me out! He was relieved at the diagnosis because he told me that he had had a chat with Dr Wallace and knew that a blockage in the bowel could be the result of a tumour. He remained in Admissions until going to surgery at 1.00 a.m.

Although we were all surprised at the diagnosis, no-one thought to question it. We were after all in hospital and in the hands of the professionals. Why would we?
Oh how we came to regret that decision!

CHAPTER 2
THE MIS-DIAGNOSIS

The following morning I visited Colin and he did not seem well at all. He said that he had not had a good night and had continued to feel sick, was unable to go to the toilet and was even finding it difficult to take fluids. I felt very concerned.

Over the next couple of days he saw several doctors, none of whom seemed unduly concerned that he was unable to have a bowel movement or eat any food. He was eventually given an enema and suppositories but to no effect. He ate one spoonful of mashed up cornflakes and drank a few sips of milk and water. He still felt nauseous. He spoke to the hospital staff and told them he felt his condition was not improving. I spoke to nurses and expressed my concern. We were both told by a doctor and nursing staff that after such an operation the bowel goes into ileus and that it would right itself naturally. By this point I was feeling very concerned. My son in law John and I went to see the Ward Sister to express our grave concerns that Colin was deteriorating and becoming dehydrated. She agreed to put up an IV drip at John's insistence and to administer an enema. She said that she had spoken to a doctor who was aware of the situation and she reiterated to us that, "nature would take its course".

It was the morning of Christmas Eve and I had accepted that Colin would be spending Christmas in hospital and I was planning to be with him. I was so shocked when I received a telephone call from him to say that he was being discharged from hospital at 3.00 pm and asking me to collect him. He said that he had seen a doctor who assured him that things would right themselves naturally. I asked him what the nurses had understood about his condition, and he replied that they had said nothing about his condition, but he knew where they were all going for Christmas, what presents they had bought and who was coming to Christmas dinner, because his bed was located near the nurses' station. I told him I was worried and that I was not sure he was fit to be discharged, and he said that perhaps when he was home and being looked after his condition would improve. Colin always sent me a Christmas bouquet and even though he was so poorly, this year was no exception and he had organised from his hospital bed for flowers to be sent to me. They arrived at the same time as he got home. The poignancy of this hit me later.

I picked Colin up from the hospital and he was given co-codamol and an out-patient appointment for six weeks later.

Whilst I am no expert it was patently obvious to me that he was a very sick man. He was like an old man walking to the car. He was so weak and tired after walking a couple of hundred yards, a distance he would normally sprint. The journey home for him was tortuous because each time the car hit a pothole or a bump in the road he winced with pain. When we arrived home he sat on the sofa and tried to sip water but he could not manage it and he said he needed a rest. A little later my brother, Brian, called to visit Colin but it was obvious he could not cope with visitors and so Brian left after a short time. He told me he thought Colin looked ill and he felt worried about him. I said that I felt the same but that hospital staff had assured us he would be fine.

We went to bed on Christmas Eve and Colin was unable to lie down. His stomach was distended and he felt nauseous. He sat upright all night and I sat up with him trying to comfort him.

On Christmas Day Colin got up but did not have enough energy to dress. This was so out of character. Colin was an extremely smart man who took a pride in his appearance but he spent the day in a towelling robe. Colin had always loved Christmas and was a very sociable and gregarious person. He loved company and always welcomed visitors with a stunning smile and a glass of wine. However, this Christmas was very different. He just lay on the sofa; he looked so ill and found it difficult to talk. As people arrived to give him presents, he just nodded and smiled. No-one stayed long because they could see that Colin was unable to cope with company. When his children and grand-children phoned to wish him a Happy Christmas, he was hardly able to speak to them. He ate nothing and sipped a little water. In the afternoon I asked if he thought I should phone the emergency doctor but he said that he had only been discharged from hospital the previous evening and was told that he needed to give things a few days to right themselves, so he really felt he had to do this. I deeply regret not ignoring his opinion and I urge anyone who feels concerned to ignore medical advice and follow their instincts because they are usually right.

Christmas night and Boxing Night were sheer hell! Colin was unable to climb the stairs to bed. He could not lie down because of the pain and discomfort in his abdomen. He slept for two nights on the sofa down-stairs propped up with duvets and pillows. He looked ill, and at this point found it difficult to sip water.

CHAPTER 3
THE TRUE DIAGNOSIS

On the 27th December, I phoned our GP, Dr Wallace, and explained that Colin had been discharged from hospital, but that I was extremely concerned about his condition. She told me to take him back to hospital straight away. This I did.

We went to the Admissions Department at the Walsgrave Hospital and the experience was the stuff of nightmares. It was an absolutely freezing day with sub zero temperatures. At Reception I explained that Colin was a hospital discharge but that he was so ill. We were told to take a seat. After about an hour Colin saw a triage nurse. I felt such a sense of relief when he went into the nurse because I believed he would now get the attention he needed as it was obvious that he was a very sick man. However, the relief turned to absolute horror when the nurse returned him to the waiting room. There were automated doors which continually opened and closed letting in the freezing temperatures. Colin sat shivering and looking near to collapse. I went to Reception on several occasions to ask when he would get a bed, and to express my concerns, only to be told they were busy and he would be seen eventually. By this time Colin was looking extremely ill, and other patients, who were ill themselves and waiting to be seen, expressed concern and urged me to get help for Colin. At this point I became very assertive and again went to Reception very loudly demanding a bed "NOW". Miraculously, that elusive bed became available. However, there was no blanket and I had to take my coat off to wrap around Colin, as he was so cold.

He eventually saw a doctor who said that he needed a drip and an X-ray and he took a blood sample. It was to be several hours before he saw a surgeon. The drip the doctor requested did not appear, and after an hour I asked where this was, only to be told they were busy. I knew Colin was completely dehydrated as he had been unable to drink for days. I demanded a drip be attached and this was reluctantly done. My daughter, Kate, and her husband John, arrived at the hospital and were shocked that Colin was shivering and did not have a blanket. John insisted that one be supplied.

Several hours later a surgeon turned up, and it was Dr Agaba, who was the doctor who had carried out Colin's first operation. He said that the problem was probably due to the fact that he had sutured too tightly on the first occasion and that this had happened in the past, or that the gauze he had used to straighten the colon was restricting it. He said that he would have to open the initial wound but that the operation would be minor and take about an hour. He said that Colin would be admitted to the ward and that the operation would take place the next day.

At about two o'clock I went to visit Colin and he told me that he would be going to surgery at 3.00 pm. We agreed that when he went to theatre I would go home and return in the evening when he would probably be feeling better. I felt relief that his pain and distress would soon be over. At about 5.30pm I telephoned the ward to check on his recovery and was told that he had not returned from theatre yet and to telephone a little later. I was not unduly concerned at this point as I assumed they were busy. I rang again at 6.30, 7.00, 8.00 and 9.00. By this time, I was beside myself with worry. I just knew something was horribly wrong. When I telephoned at 9.00 pm a nurse advised me that Colin was on his way back from theatre but that the surgeon who had undertaken the surgery, Mr Wong, wanted to speak to me in the morning. I felt an overwhelming sense of fear and panic. I telephoned my friend Mary, a nurse, and she said we should go the hospital immediately, which we did. When we arrived on the Ward, the Consultant, Mr Wong, had just left but the nurse said he would be available tomorrow. Mary was very assertive and told the nurse that we could not wait until tomorrow. She explained that she felt I had been through enough and that I needed to speak to Mr Wong tonight. The nurse said she would telephone him and Mr Wong returned to the ward to speak to us.

He said that Dr Agaba had begun the operation on Colin and then got into difficulty and called upon Mr Wong for assistance. Mr Wong opened up the abdomen across its width and found that Colin's colon was distended to three times its normal size. It was packed full of faeces, debris and infection. So much so that it had taken him two hours to clean it out. He told us it was impacted right back to the small intestine and that there was a high risk of infection because Colin had not been prepared for the surgery. Because of this he had carried out a temporary colostomy which he said was reversible.

He also told me that the cause of the obstruction was a tumour, the size of a fifty pence piece in the left hand side of the colon. He showed me photographs taken during the surgery of the distended colon and the tumour.
I listened in total disbelief. How could he have a tumour, he had absolutely no symptoms other than constipation for a few days? I felt tears roll down my face. This man was so fit, so healthy, it was impossible!

I then thought about how he had been discharged from hospital on Christmas Eve as medically fit, and with the advice that nature would take its course. I thought about the intense pain, misery and distress he had had to endure. I remembered how he had tried to smile at visitors and how he could not climb the stairs to bed, lie down or even sip water.

But most of all I remembered medical and nursing staff on the ward insisting that he was fit and that his only problem was ileus. A huge surge of anger engulfed me. These were professionals who were supposed to care for the sick, for God's sake! I remember asking Mr Wong if he had any idea how angry I felt that Walsgrave Hospital had inflicted such treatment on my beloved Colin. He nodded and said that he understood.

I asked Mr Wong not to tell Colin about the cancer immediately. He was physically so weak. He had suffered intense agony, he had undergone two major operations within a few days and he had not eaten or drank for nine days. Whilst he was psychologically a very strong character, I felt he needed to feel stronger before he was told. I also wanted to be with him when this happened. Mr Wong agreed with me that this was a good approach and said he would not tell Colin immediately. I felt very relieved at this, and also that he was now in Mr Wong's care. I felt that Mr Wong was an excellent surgeon and a caring man. He spoke to me with compassion and also gave me hope when he said he felt optimistic that the tumour had not spread. He had removed the tumour together with a sizeable piece of colon and some lymph nodes and these had been sent to histology but at this stage the prognosis looked good.

When Mr Wong left, I sat with Mary trying to take in the enormity of what had happened to Colin. How could he have cancer, he was so fit and well? Why did they not find it in the first place? Did he ever have a hernia at all? Was he misdiagnosed in the first place? It slowly began to dawn on me that he was misdiagnosed and that the wrong operation had been carried out initially, and his discharge from hospital was inappropriate and premature. I felt white rage engulf me. How could they do this to Colin? Gentle, kind, funny, loving Colin, who would never knowingly hurt any-one, was now desperately ill as a result of their actions. I again dissolved into tears as I thought about the cancer and how I would tell him.

Mary and I sat for a long time, both in tears, holding each other. I do not know how long it was before we mopped our faces and went to see Colin. He was still suffering the effects of the anaesthetic and he was drowsy but he opened his beautiful blue eyes and flashed his amazing smile.

He said, "Hello you, hello Mary Reilly," and then he drifted off back to sleep.

When we left the hospital in the early hours, we were both in a state of shock. Although Mary wanted me to go home with her, I felt I needed to be alone. I spent the night deep in thought as the reality of the situation began to hit me. Colin was such a strong character with an entirely positive outlook on life. If any-one could beat cancer Colin was the man. We always made such a good team and I told myself we could deal with this. At least we now knew what was wrong and I would soon have him home, and I would get him fit for the treatment he was going to need. I would channel the anger I felt into getting Colin well.

After a sleepless night, I went to the hospital at 8.00 am. The Ward Sister approached me and said, "God, what a man!"

She then told me that Colin had dragged himself out of bed despite the fact that he had only returned from surgery the previous night and was connected to lines, drips, drains and machinery. He had refused assistance from the nurse to wash.

When I walked behind the curtains he was trying to wash himself despite all the paraphernalia. I asked him what on earth he thought he was doing and he said he had set himself some targets to aid a speedy recovery. The first was to get out of bed this morning! He told me that the second was to be fit enough to take me out for my birthday which was in two weeks time. He told me to book a table today for whichever restaurant I wanted to go to and he would be taking me there in two weeks.

I laughed and said, "The best present will be having you home with me."

"Well, you'll get that sweetheart," was his reply.

He then told me that Dr Agaba wanted to speak to me, and I told him I had spoken to Mr Wong the previous evening.

He asked, "Did he tell you everything?"

"What's everything?" I asked.

Colin said, "I've got cancer but they think they have managed to remove it all."

I was so shocked that he had been told despite the reassurance I had been given. I asked him how he felt and he replied by saying, "It's nothing we can't handle, is it kid?"

"Of course not," I said.

He also told me that he had had a colostomy and asked me how I felt about it.

I replied, "It's nothing we can't handle, is it kid?"

He smiled.

I helped Colin to wash, and we sat talking about what had happened to him. He said he was relieved that at least he knew what he was dealing with, and felt that given time he would feel better. I felt a sense of deepening anger that my request not to tell Colin today was not honoured. I felt that at this stage he really did not need to know. He looked so ill, weak, pale and tired. What was it with this hospital??

At about 8.00 pm he suggested I go home and said we both needed to catch up on our beauty sleep. I drove home feeling more optimistic than I had for a week. Although he was clearly very poorly, the old positive attitude and strong character was showing itself. That's my Colin, I thought. The drive home gave me the opportunity to reflect on the fact that Dr Agaba had gone ahead and told Colin he had cancer, and I felt betrayed and upset. I wanted Colin home as I was beginning to feel that Walsgrave Hospital was not a good place to be. I went to bed and was so tired that I was able to fall asleep for the first time since the 18th December.

CHAPTER 4
LIFE AND DEATH IN INTENSIVE CARE

It was about 5.00 am when I was awakened by the telephone ringing.

The voice on the other end said, "This is Maria from Ward C2S. I think that you had better come to the hospital at once. Colin has crashed and he has been taken to the theatre's Intensive Treatment Unit (ITU). He is very poorly."

I put down the phone and felt an overwhelming sense of fear and terror. How could this happen, he was improving when I left the hospital? I did not telephone anyone, I never even thought about it. I threw on a jogging suit, jumped in the car and raced to the hospital. When I got to the ward, Maria took me to the theatre ITU. My precious Colin was surrounded by staff, he was wired up to so much technology and wearing a mask to assist him breathing. He saw me and smiled.
He pulled the mask from his face and whispered, "Don't worry kid, it's just a hiccup."

But I was worried. I was absolutely terrified. This did not look like a hiccup to me. The love of my life was so ill. How could this fit and healthy individual be so desperately ill? He only went into hospital because he had constipation. He had never really been ill in his life. An ITU doctor and nurse continually monitored him and I just could not take in what was happening to him. I felt so shocked and frightened. The doctor told me that Colin was a very sick man and that they were doing tests to find out what had happened but he said there were three possibilities – he may have suffered a heart attack, there may be a blood clot on his lung or he may have a massive infection. I was informed that they would move him to an intensive care ward as soon as a bed became available and this was likely to be a little later in the morning.

At 11.00 am Colin was moved to the 5th Floor ITU and I realised just how ill he was when four members of the medical team accompanied him on the short journey in the lift to the 5th floor. He was settled in and I asked a nurse whether they had confirmed what had actually caused Colin to become so ill. I told her the doctor said there were three possibilities. She said that she had been told Colin was "Septic".

I felt confused and frightened. I telephoned Sarah, Colin's daughter and she said she would come from Derbyshire straightaway. I told Colin she was on her way and he was so pleased but he was concerned that his little grandchildren Kyle and Lauren should not see him in his current state connected to all the technology. He thought it might have a negative impact on them and cause them to worry. After some soul searching Sarah decided to bring the children and make the decision when she got here. In the event, once he knew they were in the hospital, he wanted to see them, and they wanted to see him and there was no problem. Thankfully they spent some time with him before he died.

Throughout the day Colin struggled on with his assisted breathing machine. He was able to communicate with me by hand signs or by moving the mask and whispering some words. At one point he touched my hand and pointed to the man in the bed directly opposite who was surrounded by relatives. I turned to look and when I looked back Colin gave me the thumbs down sign. The man died a couple of hours later. I gently squeezed Colin's hand but now I often wonder what thoughts must have been going through his mind and if he knew he was going to die and it fills me with sadness.

Colin became increasingly tired as he was expending so much energy in trying to breathe. He tried to write things down but his writing just trailed away. He gave my daughter, Kate, a note and all she could decipher was foxes and video. She had no idea what he was trying to say, but nodded reassuringly so that he thought she understood. A few nights later when we got home from hospital she switched on the television and there was a programme about foxes. She suddenly jumped up and said, "Mum, that's what Colin was saying, he wanted us to record this programme for him."

Although it was half way through she recorded what remained. He loved all wild-life programmes and we thought it would be good for him to watch when he was recovering at home. Although physically he was very poorly and weak, it gave a clear indication that his mind was working over time. He also asked Phillip, his son in law, to move his car from the kerb and onto the drive because the tax was due shortly. At the end of the day the nurse told me he was doing well and although I did not think he looked good, I was relieved by her reassurances. I went home late evening and thought perhaps we had turned a corner.

On the 31st December, I went into the hospital early in the morning and Colin did not look well at all. He seemed to be struggling with the mask and his breathing was very laboured. The mask was of a rigid construction and it had cut into the bridge of his nose leaving an ugly looking wound on his skin. He was finding it difficult to communicate with me although he struggled to do so. He attempted sign language but the effort was too great. He tried to write but he was too weak and the writing was illegible. When I could not understand he became frustrated and fractious which was so unlike the real Colin. He always had endless patience with me. I became very anxious and confused.

At about 7.00 pm, I popped home to have a shower and a short break. I arrived back at the hospital just before ten and a doctor was waiting to speak to me. He told me that they were concerned that Colin's breathing was deteriorating and that they were going to put him on a ventilator to give his lungs a rest. I just could not believe it, how could Colin be going on a life support machine? He had come into hospital for a minor complaint and life support machines were for victims of terrible trauma, weren't they?

I went to Colin who was struggling to breathe and his eyes looked so troubled, but he could not communicate with me. I explained to him that the doctors were going to sedate him so that his lungs could have a little rest. He blinked to let me know he understood. I told him I would be there when he woke up again and he blinked in reply.

That was the last time I spoke to my beloved Colin while he was conscious. It never occurred to me that he would die. The doctor did not warn me that this was a distinct possibility.

Because doctors work in this environment, there appears to be an assumption that you understand what intensive care is all about, but how could you? Fortunately, most people will never set foot inside an intensive care unit. I feel that had I known the probable outcome that last conversation with Colin would have been so very different and I felt a sense of anger and sadness for Colin and myself. Our relationship had always been one in which we talked openly about our feelings and I feel that the opportunity to say our last goodbyes was denied to us. The sadness of this will live with me forever.

Colin was put on a respirator and Kate and I went in to see him. I looked at him, motionless, dependant upon technology and I was convinced he would not survive through the night.

Kate persuaded me to go home as there was nothing more we could do. The nurses advised that this was the best course of action because if there were any changes they would phone me whatever the time. We went home and I lay awake all night praying that the phone would not ring.

It was such a relief when it was seven in the morning and the phone had not rung. At least Colin was no worse!

Kate and I went straight to the hospital and sat by Colin's bedside. I could not believe that the man I loved was totally inanimate and unable to communicate with me. I spoke to him but did not know if he could hear me. I thought perhaps he could because I had been told that hearing is the last sense to go.

I am blessed because I have an amazing family and friends and between them they ensured I was never at the hospital alone. Kate moved in with me. All were shocked and devastated at the turn of events. Colin was probably the fittest and healthiest in our circle and here he was attached to a ventilator.

I sat by Colin's bed willing him to live. I reminded him of all the plans we had made for our retirement and told him he had better get well. I was overcome with the most crippling fear.

Although not religious I went to the hospital chapel and prayed. I made all kinds of bargains with God, but God wasn't listening. I tried to contact Colin's son, Tim, who lived in Hong Kong but was unable to do so as he was on holiday and had no idea of his father's condition. Again that night I went to bed with an awful sense of fear and impending doom. Morning arrived without the phone call and the sense of relief was overwhelming but I experienced the most terrible crippling sadness and loneliness. This was not the New Year we had planned.

It occurred to me that when Colin woke up, he would want to know what had happened whilst he was unconscious, so I decided to keep a journal so that I would be able to relate what had happened to him. I recorded the weather, the people who had sat with him and all the people who continually phoned to ask about his welfare. I wrote down all the significant things that were happening to him and I wrote down my feelings. It helped me feel closer to him because I knew that one day soon I would be sharing these thoughts with him.

On the 2nd January, Tim had returned from holiday and telephoned. I told him what had happened. He was obviously upset and was going to fly straight over to England, but after speaking to the doctor, it was decided that it was best to leave it until his father was taken off the ventilator because that is when Colin would benefit most from his company. In the event, he came for his father's funeral.

The next day when Kate and I arrived at the hospital, it was like a physical blow when the nurse told us that Colin's oxygen levels were poor and that the antibiotics were failing to move the infection from his chest. At this point I believed he was going to die but I dared not admit it even to myself.

Brian and Val were with me when a Roman Catholic priest turned up. He asked if he could give Colin the Last Rites. Colin was not a practising Catholic and several months earlier we had watched a programme on the television about near death experiences. One man who was interviewed said that when he was lying in hospital unable to communicate, a priest had turned up to administer the last rites. He said this had really frightened him because he believed he was about to die. Colin had laughed and said, "If I am ever in that position, do not let one of them near me!"

I relayed this conversation to the priest who said he understood and he would say prayers for healing. I told the priest to go ahead and administer the Last Rites because I decided that we needed all the help we could get and took advantage of his being unconscious!

The nurse told me I was spending too much time at the hospital and that I needed to conserve my energy for the time when Colin was conscious because that was when he would need me most. But how do you leave? How do you walk away? What if he opens his eyes? What if he dies? My friends Mary, Ann and Gill were there at the hospital, and of course the wonderful Kate. All said that the nurse was right and to try to go to the hospital a little later each morning. I spoke to Sarah and she also felt this was sensible. Sarah again came to see her father and brought her sister Fiona.

I continued to talk to Colin and tell him what was happening. I told him that his sisters phoned from Ireland every day and that Masses were being said the length and breadth of the land to pray for his recovery. I told him the phone never stopped ringing with people who were concerned. I told him that Tim was coming to see him and I told him what Manchester United were up to, but there was never a response.

As time went by I was so relieved that Colin was still with me. It was becoming clear that Colin's condition was originally misdiagnosed and I was experiencing such a mixture of emotions that it was difficult to think straight. One day, Dr Agaba, who originally diagnosed and operated on Colin for a supposed hernia came to see me. He told me that Colin was one of the nicest men he had met and that he could not believe he was on a ventilator. He told me that if there was any justice he would pull through and that God was good. He told me to pray!

I felt angry and Kate sensing my rising anger took over and stopped me losing my cool. She asked him lots of questions to which he went and found the answers. He came on other occasions to talk to me. I felt that he was suffering, and the compassionate part of me felt sad, but then I thought about the unnecessary surgery, the horrendously painful Christmas and the long term damage done to poor Colin, and my compassion quickly dissipated.

On the 3rd January we arrived at the hospital to be told that Colin was not absorbing food and had a high temperature. A nurse called Danny was looking after Colin. He was calm, caring and competent. He asked me to tell him a little about Colin because he explained that in the ITU he never really got to know his patients as they were not conscious. I told him all about Colin and ended by saying that he would not be pleased with his appearance. He was such a smart man and had a wonderful head of thick white hair which he washed every day, but here it was looking greasy and unkempt. Danny told me to go for a coffee which I did. When I got back, he had washed Colin's hair. He said he was not much of a stylist but at least it was clean. It looked wonderful as far as I was concerned. I felt very touched that some-one so young could understand how important this was to me and how touched Colin would be when I told him. Another young female nurse came and sat beside me one day and held my hand. We sat talking about Colin and looking at him when she remarked what a handsome man he was. It was little acts of kindness such as this that made life bearable in ITU.

I sat holding Colin's hand and telling him he had to fight a little harder and that I loved him and needed him to talk to me. He looked so peaceful. If he had not been connected to all the technology, I would have expected him to wake up at any moment. If only he could.

The 4th January was an eventful day. I had made the decision to arrive at the hospital a little later in the morning and leave a little earlier in the evening so that I could conserve my energy for when Colin regained consciousness. Sarah and Fiona again visited and we were all longing for some good news, no matter how small. I was beginning to feel exhausted and very down. I could not eat or sleep and I was living on my nerves.

Mr Wong arrived and spent a long time with Colin. He then asked to see me. I felt blind panic. I felt he was going to tell me something awful. He then told me we could start to feel optimistic. He said the infection was getting under control. He told me that the infection had affected Colin's heart, lungs and kidneys but that everything was now improving. He said the only problem was that he was not absorbing food but he thought that if the food was changed, the problem would resolve. He said that the rubbish which had been left in Colin's colon after the first operation had caused the infection.

I felt such as sense of relief, as though someone had lifted a ten ton weight from my shoulders. The knot in my stomach loosened slightly. I still felt as though I was on the precipice but that I was not quite so near the edge. I related the information to Sarah and Fiona who were relieved and elated.

I phoned Bri and Val, Kate and my mum - we were all in tears. I left the hospital that night, and after having dinner with Mary and her husband Pete, I went home and felt that I would sleep but it was impossible. This was the first night I could believe that the phone was not going to ring.

Next day when I got to the hospital, it was good news. The doctor told me that today they intended to reduce Colin's sedation and that he would slowly regain consciousness. I remember having mixed feelings. On the one hand I felt excited that he would be coming back to me but on the other I was frightened about how ill he might be. I telephoned Sarah, his sisters in Ireland and his son Tim and gave them the good news. All were overjoyed. I felt that at least today there was a little chink of light in the darkness. I tried to be a little more optimistic but being surrounded by such negativity had taken its toll and it was difficult to be upbeat. I left the hospital at tea-time and went for a meal with my family. I later returned to kiss Colin goodnight and as I looked at him I allowed myself to feel positive. I felt that at least he was on his way back to me. The night was endless, it seemed to last forever. I just wanted to be at the hospital in case he opened his eyes and I was not there.

Kate and I got to the hospital and both of us felt a little easier. I prayed that today was the day that Colin opened his eyes. The Ward Sister approached me and I felt the most gut-wrenching pain when she said that Colin's kidneys were not functioning properly. She told me that all his sedation and painkillers had been stopped but he was failing to regain consciousness as expected. She told me rather brutally that the toxin levels were still high and that he would need another drug, but if that failed he would need dialysis. She went on to say that when patients are given dialysis they can "crash". I could no longer contain the tears. All those that had been bottled up just streamed down my face as the absolute horror, disappointment and fear of the situation hit me.

Kate held me in her arms and tried to be positive. She reminded me of Mr Wong's words, "there will be good days and there will be bad ones ahead." The Sister said that a doctor would review the situation. I was engulfed by misery and terror. The doctor decided that Colin's kidneys were processing the toxins very slowly and that he might take several days to regain consciousness. The doctor was kind and sensitive and this is so important in ITU, when the person you adore is on life support your emotions are on a roller coaster. All your fears and anxieties are near the surface. I listened to every word, I watched for every bit of body language, I read between the lines and my senses were on red alert.

Things change from minute to minute, hour to hour, and changes in my emotions coincided with changes in Colin's condition. A machine bleeped and I jumped. I became an expert at reading all the technology and reading people's faces. I lived on my nerves and the only thing that kept me going was the fact that I needed to be there for the man I loved.

Over the next few days we waited for Colin to regain consciousness but he still lay there motionless. I found it hard to believe that he was still so unaware that we were all waiting for him. I felt devastation and I kept asking myself how this could have happened. He was never ill; he was so fit and healthy. Immediately before his admission to hospital he was planning a fabulous retirement. I knew he must be fighting desperately to live. He loved life so much; there was so much to live for. We had all our plans, hopes and dreams.

He had his grandchildren whom he loved dearly and he was expecting a new grandchild in the summer. No, I told myself, he would not give up easily; he would be fighting like hell! I willed him to live and told him I loved him and that I did not want a call in the night!

The following day a doctor told me that Colin needed to go to theatre today to undergo a tracheotomy. I asked him how he thought Colin's body could withstand any more and he said that I needed to see this in a positive light. He said that Colin's mouth was breaking down and that the tube needed to be removed. He said that when Colin awoke it would be less traumatic as he would not have the discomfort of a tube down his throat. I had the most awful misgivings but was told I needed to trust their professional judgement. Sarah and Ann were with me and it was a very emotional afternoon as we had to watch as another family were told their father's ventilator was going to be switched off. Their distress and grief was tangible and almost too much to bear. We all felt caught up in the maelstrom of their emotion. I felt absolute compassion for the pain they were suffering but I am ashamed to say I also thought, Thank God it's not my Colin. I was frozen with fear and unable to offer any consolation. This was the reality of life in the intensive care unit. During Colin's stay I had already seen three people die and prayed that Colin would not be the fourth.

Colin eventually went to theatre at 7.00 pm and I was told it was a quick procedure and he would be back in half an hour. I watched him go and sat with Mary in the relative's room to anxiously await his return. The first hour was just about bearable but then I was unable to contain my fears. I walked up and down the corridor and then began to cry inconsolably. I believed that Colin was not coming back to me. When I could stand it no longer Mary asked the nurse where Colin was and she said he was on his way back. He eventually arrived back at 10.00 pm. His mouth was contorted where the tubes had been, but at least he was alive. I felt so alone and I missed Colin so much. I was worried that I was leaning on Kate too much. She was a rock and always there for me but she was so young and it seemed so unfair. I would normally have discussed such things with Colin but of course Colin was not there!

The next day was perhaps the most memorable of all. Amongst the "worst" days it rated highly but it was also a day that gave me great hope. When I arrived at the hospital I entered the lift with a really bad feeling and a sense of foreboding. The nurse told me that Mr Wong wanted to speak to me. I felt a sense of impending doom. I knew it was going to be bad news because the nurse avoided eye contact with me. On previous days she had been very chatty but today she was avoiding any contact with me. I was to meet Mr Wong at 2.00 pm.

I went to speak to Colin, and for the first time his eyes flickered. I was filled with joy because this was the first reaction I had had from him. I told him I needed him to respond, I needed him back. I told him how much I loved him and his fingers flickered on mine. I felt tears of joy run down my face. I just knew in my heart he was on the way back to me. A nurse told me that when she was attending to him she asked him if he wanted Kath and his eyes were flickering and when she said this I experienced a sense of elation. It felt so good to know that he was aware of my presence. Everyone who visited him talked to him and got some small response. A lot of joyful tears were shed.

However, at two o'clock my friend Ann came with me to see Mr Wong. The tears of joy soon dissipated only to be replaced by despair when he spoke to me. He told me that Colin's results were back from histology and that it was not good news. Mr Wong is a caring and compassionate man who told me with honesty, gentleness and sensitivity that Colin's prognosis was not good. Results showed that Colin had a form of cancer, which had an average life expectancy of five years. As the news began to slowly sink in, the enormity of what he was saying hit me. He said he had a window of three months in which to get Colin well enough for chemotherapy. I looked at Mr Wong in total disbelief.

Colin's body had been ravaged by two operations in the space of a week, a huge infection, and two weeks on a life support machine. He was being pumped full of toxins so how on earth could he face chemotherapy and yet more toxins. I felt a huge wave of despair engulf me. Then suddenly the despair was replaced by cold, white anger. If he had been diagnosed correctly initially, he would only have one fight on his hands, now he had two. I asked Mr Wong if he knew how angry I was feeling and he nodded. I told him to get Colin conscious so that he was aware that he had a flight on his hands. I just could not believe the cruelty of the situation and I cried all afternoon. But as I looked at Colin lying there utterly helpless, I knew the crying had to stop. He was fighting so hard to come back to us and so I owed it to him to start fighting too. The anger returned and I was determined to use this as a positive force. In the past, when I used to get angry about things Colin would respond by saying, "Don't get mad, get even".

I determined that when Colin was better, then I would deal with the hospital. In the meantime, all my energies would be used to get him well. He always said we made a great team, now we would prove it. I told Mr Wong that Colin was a very strong character and a born fighter and that if any-one could beat this, it was Colin, and he could add to this the fact that we were the strongest of teams. I told him to give Colin back his consciousness and we would do the rest. I sat by Colin's bed with my friend Gill, and as we sat and talked Colin's eyes flickered. When I held his hand, I asked if he could hear me and his eyes flickered in response. When I held his hand, he gripped mine gently. I knew he was almost back with me but more importantly he knew that he was not alone.

When Kate and I arrived at the hospital on the 9th January, Brian and Val were with him and they said they were concerned about Colin's breathing. They felt it had changed. A doctor told me that Colin's tracheotomy was not working properly and that the incision was too small and they needed to re-do it in order to make a larger

incision. I could barely believe what I was hearing. I looked at the doctor and remember saying,
"How much more do you think his body can take?"

He told me there was no choice and that it had to be done. A consultant was called to the ITU and did the procedure on Colin there and then. He told me everything was fine and the procedure had gone well. I felt cold and shivery and on the verge of collapse. I just so longed to speak to Colin, my best friend, my soul mate, the other half of me but he was inanimate. How did the arch communicator come to be silenced like this? I kept asking myself how this could have happened. I begged Colin to speak to me but there was no response. I begged God to let Colin speak to me but again there was no response.

On the 10th January we were told that things were looking bad for Colin. His kidneys were not working, his oxygen levels were poor and he was not responding. I thought, My God, he's going to die! The doctor continued to speak to my brother and I, and I remember interrupting him and asking directly
"Is he going to die?"
I asked again, "Is he going to die?"
The doctor replied, "Well, it's 50/50."
I asked again, "Is he going to die?"
He said, "It is likely, yes."

I felt very sick and began to cry. My worst nightmare was being realised, the love of my life was slipping away. I could hear Brian asking questions but none of them registered with me. I remember other people coming to the hospital. I remember seeing Kate, John, Matt my son, but I don't know what else happened.

I was in a state of shock. Although I had feared this outcome, I had never let myself believe it would really happen. I went to Colin and kissed and cuddled him. I begged him not to die and leave me. I can remember my son in law, John, putting his arms around me and telling me to let him go. I knew he was right. Colin had fought long and hard and if he could have stayed he would certainly have done so now.

That evening I sat with family and friends in the visitors' room waiting for Mr Wong. The atmosphere was taut with tension. It was like a condemned man waiting for death. Mr Wong arrived with the ITU Consultant. I was hearing the words I prayed would never be spoken. Mr Wong told me that my beloved Colin was going to die. He said that it was unlikely that he would survive the night. He said something had happened to his body the previous day and he was not sure what. In effect it was shutting down and he was suffering from Adult Respiratory Distress Syndrome (ARDS).

He had fought so desperately to live, he loved life so much. Only two days before we were told that he was improving and that we could begin to feel more positive, but now we were being told that his life was ebbing away. I felt an over-riding sense of shock. How could this be happening to Colin? He was never ill. He was so fit and healthy. He was so alive and now they were telling me he was about to die. I kept telling myself no, no, no, not Colin.

I looked at those in the room and their faces confirmed what I did not want to know. I then heard the gentle voice of Mr Wong breaking into my thoughts. He told me that there was one more thing they could try. This was to

change Colin's ventilator to a different type which actually shakes the body and he may respond. I thought of all that Colin's poor body had undergone since the 17th December and I could not bear the thought of it being shaken. It is so difficult when you have a loved one in ITU because you do not know how much they are aware of and it makes decisions so hard to make. I remember saying to Mr Wong,
"No, just leave him alone. He cannot endure any more."

At this point my brother became upset and told me that Colin had to be given every chance no matter how small. Everyone in the room agreed with Brian, and I felt that perhaps they were right because Colin had never been a quitter and so how could I give up on him now. Colin was a born motivator and he was always full of encouragement to others. I thought of his favourite expression, "Go for it!" and so I told Mr Wong to do just that. Mr Wong explained that they would know within a few hours whether Colin was responding. He suggested that I went home and they would phone me when they needed me.

I don't recall the journey home. Kate was with me as always and I felt unable to function or even think clearly. At 5.00 am the telephone rang and a gentle Scottish voice said,
"Kath, you need to come to the hospital, Colin has not responded. You need to contact the rest of the family."

CHAPTER 5
SAYING GOODBYE

It was a very dark, icy January morning with sub zero temperatures. I remember thinking that Colin loved the sunshine and warmth and so this was a horrible morning on which to die. I asked the nurse to phone his beloved Sarah, so that his daughters could come and say their goodbyes. I prayed they would arrive in time. The road conditions were treacherous and they had to drive down the motorway from Derbyshire.

I sat by his bed and held his hand as I had always done; I kissed him gently and told him I would love him forever. I became conscious of people arriving at the hospital. My brother, my nephew Dave, my son Mat, our dear friends Mary and Pete, and Ann followed shortly. I looked at them and felt confused and bewildered. What were all these people doing at the hospital at this time in the morning? Then it suddenly occurred to me – they had come to say their goodbyes. The realisation was like a physical blow. It confirmed that my darling Colin was going to die.

The nurse asked me several times when Colin's daughters would arrive. I explained they had a long way to come and when he said he hoped they would arrive in time I knew death was imminent. I took Colin in my arms and asked him to hang on until Sarah arrived, but I knew time was running out. One by one, people came to say goodbye and although it was heartbreaking it was comforting to know he was so dearly loved.

The nurse told me that Tim, Colin's son, was on the telephone from Hong Kong and I spoke to him and had to tell him that his father was about to die. It was very sad and Tim asked me to tell him he loved him. This made me cry because I knew Colin would have so loved to hear the words from Tim's lips himself.

I went back to Colin and held him. Brian, Kate and John were with him, as well as Ann. There was little dignity on the ward. All that separated us from everyone else were flimsy curtains. Whilst we were talking to Colin, the curtains at the end of the bed opened and there stood Dr Agaba. I felt an overwhelming sense of rage. How dare this person intrude on our last moments together, hadn't he done enough already? I suddenly felt the urge to hit out at him but I felt my brother's arms hold me back as he said, "Not now – we'll deal with him later".

I saw Kate get up and go outside of the curtains. I later discovered that she had told the Sister to keep him out of my way, as I held him responsible for Colin's death and she felt if he reappeared I would not be responsible for my actions.
Everyone then left me alone with Colin and I told him he could let go, he had fought enough. I thanked him for all

the wonderful gifts he had given me, not least his everlasting love.

I promised him then that whatever happened I would find out the truth and I would ensure that justice was done and seen to be done.

I heard foot-steps running along the corridor and a scream, the curtains opened and there were Sarah and Fiona, who had made the frantic dash from Derbyshire to be with their father. The nurse had phoned them twice on their mobile to say that time was running out. They were so frightened he would slip away without them. Colin hung on to life long enough for them to say their goodbyes. He died shortly afterwards at 11.20 am in our arms, and I like to think that he knew that in his final moments he was surrounded by love.

Following Colin's death, we all sat in the relatives' room trying to make sense of what had happened. It was impossible to believe that Colin was dead. It felt surreal. I looked out of the window down onto the road and saw all the cars and people going about their business. I could not grasp how life was going on as normal. Colin had just died! I wanted to scream.

The nurse had told me that they were preparing Colin, and I could go back into him in a few minutes. I never quite understood what "preparing" meant but I was too shocked to ask. After about 15 minutes I went back in to find that all the equipment and technology had been removed from his body including the tracheotomy tube. They had dressed him in a blue garment that was made of "J-cloth" type material, but the ultimate indignity was the frill around the neck. Colin was always so smart, he would have hated this although he would probably have laughed about it. I looked at Colin and knew instantly that his spirit had left. The body did not even look like Colin. I left the room feeling total desolation.

Danny, the nurse who had cared for Colin so lovingly, put his arms around me to comfort me and to say how sad he felt. It was a great comfort. I have nothing but praise for the nurses in intensive care; they were true professionals who undertook their role with compassion and dedication and were so different from the nurses on the surgical ward.

As I was about to leave the hospital, a nurse told me that I could collect Colin's death certificate later in the day when it had been signed by a doctor. I never collected that death certificate because I knew Colin should not be dead and so began the fight for justice for a very special human being.

I left hospital in a state of shock. I could not comprehend what was happening. I kept asking myself had Colin just died. It was an icy January day with sub zero temperatures and the weather reflected my feelings. I was frozen inside and out. I walked into the house and experienced a feeling of total emptiness – it no longer felt like my home. I sat in the lounge listening to Kate making telephone calls informing people of Colin's death. I listened in disbelief and struggled to accept that Colin had died even though I had just identified his body.

One of the phone calls made was to my boss and friend, Ron Watkins. Ron asked to speak to me. He expressed his deep sorrow and gave me advice which proved to be priceless. He told me not to collect the death certificate

from the hospital but to write to the Coroner outlining all my concerns about the care Colin had received.
Ron said, "I know this is difficult but you need to do this NOW and you need to fax it urgently to the Coroner."
I began to cry.
Ron continued, "Come on sweetheart, it's for Colin, you can do it!"

He somehow gave me the strength to do something positive. I pulled myself together and went to the computer. I wrote that letter to the Coroner, in which I stated,
"I wish to make you aware that I have grave concerns about what happened during Colin's initial stay in hospital from 17-24 December and the inaccurate diagnosis of his medical condition, and his inappropriate and premature discharge, which I believe led to his death."

Kate phoned the Coroner's office, got the fax number and sent the letter.

I will be eternally grateful to Ron Watkins for his support and wise words, because I believe that without them, the mistakes made by Walsgrave hospital would have been cremated!

The following morning I received a telephone call from the Coroner's Officer. He said the Coroner had received my letter, had read some of the hospital notes and spoken to a doctor. He said that he shared my concerns about what had happened. He went on to say that he believed there should be a post mortem examination but that this should be undertaken in a different hospital to ensure independence. He asked how I would feel about Colin's body being taken to the Leicester Royal Infirmary. I was relieved, I felt at last someone was listening to me and I might get the answers I sought, and desperately needed. The Coroner's Officer had a gentle and kind approach and this made me cry. I spent the rest of the day imagining Colin's lonely journey to Leicester and I was engulfed by deep sadness. The last time he went to Leicester was with me to buy a new outfit. It had been such a happy day buying clothes and sharing a delicious Italian lunch. It was so difficult to make sense of it all.

A couple of days later, I received a telephone call from the Coroner's Officer. He told me that the post mortem had been completed and that the Coroner shared my concerns. He said that there needed to be an Inquest and that it was in the public interest that it be heard in front of a Jury. I asked if I needed legal representation and was told this was not necessary as an Inquest is not adversarial, but rather a fact finding exercise in which all involved presents the facts to the Coroner, to enable him to reach a decision. At this stage I felt that I could represent myself anyway, as I had been with Colin throughout and had all the facts. He explained to me that the Inquest would have to be opened and then adjourned whilst he gathered all the necessary information and that a date would be arranged for the hearing when everything was to hand. He also advised me that an interim death certificate would be issued to enable the funeral to go ahead and that I would need to register the death. The date for this was my birthday, January 15th. Colin always had good timing! I registered his death with Tim, who had flown over for the funeral.

The morning of the funeral was positively Dickensian; it was a grey, gloomy, dreary January day but the service was so uplifting and reflected Colin's personality. His little grandchildren read a poem they had written. Tim and Ann spoke movingly and with great affection about Colin and his life. The hymns were uplifting and as we left the church Nat King Cole sang "Unforgettable," which indeed he was. This was the first tape Colin ever bought me, so it was the only choice. The church was full to capacity with standing room only and he was surrounded by flowers and love. He would have enjoyed it!

CHAPTER 6
WHERE TO BEGIN?

The funeral over, life became a desolate place. I just could not believe I would never see my precious Colin again. I was unable to sleep. Some nights I literally never closed my eyes. I became totally exhausted and found it difficult to function.

Some days I cried non-stop and felt that life was totally meaningless. I genuinely wanted to die. I felt physically ill and experienced all kinds of symptoms. I could not contemplate a future without my dearest Colin. I felt that I had lost my future. All the plans we had made for our retirement were lost forever. I longed to see his beautiful face, to hear his laugh, to feel his touch. I felt anxious about everything no matter how small. I just knew life would never be the same again. Eventually I visited my GP and got some sleeping tablets, and after a few nights sleep I began to feel a little stronger. My thoughts had a little more clarity and I decided I had an Inquest to face and I could not let Colin down. It was my responsibility to right the wrong.

It was difficult to know where to begin and what to do to make myself stronger. I am blessed with an amazing family and friends who all said they would support me whichever path I chose to follow. Mat, my son, came and did all the jobs around the house and changed the locks so I felt more secure. Kate, Sarah, Mary and Ann made it clear they were there for me any time of the night or day should I need them and I often did! Mary made sure I ate. All this enabled me to think about what course of action I needed to take.

Fortunately most people will never have to consider Inquests and taking on the might of the local Hospital Trust, and so when something happens, how do you know where do you begin?

Well meaning people told me that I could not take on the Trust and win and that it would all end in tears for me. Others said it was wise to look after myself, to put the trauma behind me and just move on! How could I move on if I hadn't done right by Colin? But worst of all were those who looked at me patronisingly and said such things as, "these things happen, it's no-ones fault," and who clearly felt I was a neurotic widow who needed someone to blame for her husband's death. Deep in my heart, I knew that if this had happened to me rather than Colin, he would have fought like a lion until the end for justice, and there was no choice; the battle began.

However, at this point I did not know it would be such a monumental one. For most of my professional life I had worked in a job where colleagues had integrity, professionalism and respect and I was of the mistaken opinion that all those who worked in the medical profession shared these ethics. I soon found this to be otherwise.

After considering how to proceed I felt that getting the medical records was probably the best option initially. I phoned the Legal Department at the hospital and asked how to access these. I was advised that I needed to complete a request form and write a covering letter requesting their release and they sent this to me in the post. Two weeks later I received a telephone call from the Legal Department saying the notes could be collected from them.

Accompanied by Gill, I went to the hospital and was handed the notes by a young woman who gave us assurances that they were complete and that nothing had been removed. I left the hospital and went directly to my friend Mary. As she was in the medical profession, I knew she would be able to understand the technical information and explain it to me.

She systematically went through the records and became angry. She asked me if they had said the notes were complete and I confirmed that they did. She was furious, Colin was her dear friend and she wanted some honesty. She told me that several items were missing from the notes. She identified that the following items were missing:

1. The nursing notes from Colin's first admission
2. The histology report
3. The photographs shown to us by Mr Wong following Colin's second operation
4. The radiology reports
5. The operation notes

I felt incensed. How dare they lie to me? Gill and I had been assured that the notes were complete. At this stage I could not decide whether this was due to rampant incompetence and inefficiency or something much more worrying.

I wrote to the hospital asking for access to ALL of Colin's medical records in line with the Data Protection Act. I said that if items had been removed I wanted to be informed as to what they were, and why this had happened. A week later I had not heard from the hospital and so I telephoned the Legal Department. I spoke to the woman who had told us the records were complete. She said that she owed me an apology and that she had personally removed Colin's blood test results from the records. (This was the same woman who had assured us the records were complete initially). I asked her why she had done this, and she said she thought they were too technical for me to understand. I am sure my reply can be imagined!!! She then advised me she was still unable to locate the missing items but said she would continue to search for them.

Two weeks later there was still no reply from the hospital. Gill suggested that rather than telephone, we actually go there and confront them. We did this, and were given a bundle of notes which was almost as big as the original file already in my possession. However, we were advised that the radiology reports and X-rays, operation notes and photographs were still unavailable. We were advised by the young woman in the Legal Section that she would speak to the Consultant's secretary and see if she could locate them. Gill insisted she did this in our presence. She said she would have the information the following day and that she would phone me. I reminded her that under the

Data Protection Act, the hospital had 40 days to provide me with complete and accurate records. Gill asked her to arrange a meeting with Mr Wong, the Consultant. She agreed to do this and let me know the outcome. Next day she telephoned to say that the records were still not available. Again I reminded her that under the Data Protection Act, time was running out for Walsgrave Hospital. She told me to phone her the following day and when I did she said that the radiology reports could be collected. I went to collect these and discovered that the X-rays taken on both of Colin's admissions were missing. She again said she would try to locate these. I explained that I had an appointment with a solicitor the following day. I also told her that the hospital was on day 37 of their 40 days and if they failed to conform, I would invoke the law. Later that day I had a call from the hospital to advise me that the X-rays had been located and would be ready for me to collect in a couple of days. When I went to collect them I was told they were still not available. However, at this point, I did feel that I had extracted all the other records but I was worn down. All this turmoil was a time when I was least able to deal with it. It gave me some insight into the difficult time that lay ahead if I continued to pursue this course of action. I had a good cry and told Gill I did not know if I had the strength to continue.

She replied simply, "But you can't stop, can you?"

Of course, I knew she was right.

When I had time to reflect, I was shocked how difficult the hospital had made the whole exercise and this was only the first step. It was such an ordeal and I wondered what it must be like for those who struggle without the support of friends and family. Or how do the elderly, disabled, less assertive or less articulate fare. I think the sad truth is, they do not fare well, and that many hospital mistakes are buried, literally.

I found it emotionally distressing and totally exhausting at a time when my resources were so low. I started to question whether the obstacles placed before me formed part of a strategy for wearing patients and their families down, in an attempt to discourage them from proceeding, or whether they were just supremely inefficient.

Whatever the answer, the truth is that the process certainly has the effect of wearing people down to the point that they withdraw and sadly fall at the first hurdle. To continue you need resilience, stamina and emotional energy at a time when these very qualities are at their most depleted. Collecting this information is the corner-stone of any case against the hospital and if it is just too difficult an exercise it may be necessary at this point to consult a lawyer with Medical Negligence expertise.

CHAPTER 7
THE ROCKY ROAD TO INQUEST

The Coroner had determined that an Inquest should to take place, and because of the public interest, this needed to be heard in front of a Jury. This felt daunting as it seemed a very formal and legal process. The Coroner's Officer explained to me that an Inquest is a fact finding exercise, and as such is non adversarial, and because of this she explained that I would not need legal representation. The process was outlined to me and I was advised that I needed to make a statement in writing and submit it to the Coroner, and I should also obtain statements from any other family members and friends who I felt could contribute, and who could be called to give evidence at the actual Inquest. It was explained to me that the hospital would also be instructed to submit statements from relevant members of staff, and when all of these were in the hands of the Coroner, each party would be given the others' statements so that they could read them prior to the Inquest.

I discussed the situation with my friends and family, and it was decided that statements would be written by John, my son-in-law, Brian, my brother, and my friend Mary, because these people were pivotal as they saw a great deal of Colin and were aware of the happenings in Walsgrave Hospital. I was distraught, and the thought of reliving all the events through the writing of the statement was terrifying.

However, I knew that this was the only way of getting the answers I sought about Colin's death. When he was in hospital I had kept a journal of events and so I had all the information to hand, it was just coping with it all emotionally that was problematic. I made several abortive attempts that ended in torrents of tears and much pain. I realised I was getting nowhere fast and I set myself a goal that I would complete this by the following weekend because I had to do it for Colin, and I knew in my heart he would be telling me to just get on with it! In the event, I sat up throughout that night, and by morning I had written an eight page statement outlining all the events. John, Brian and Mary also wrote theirs, and we handed them to the Coroner on the 2nd February and we were advised that the Inquest was likely to take place in early April. It was a really emotional time for all of us and it was daunting to know that we would also have to give evidence.

I had also asked the Coroner's Officer to forward me a copy of the Post Mortem report when it was available. I felt that there would be information in it which I would need to prepare for the Inquest. She did not ask me any questions or advise that I may find this difficult. If you have never been involved in a sudden death, you have absolutely no idea what a Post Mortem report contains, and I feel strongly that the Coroner's Officer should explain this before sending one out in the post. When the report arrived, I opened it and began to read and the impact it had upon me was shocking. It obviously goes into graphic detail about the process, and body parts, and I had no idea at the level of mutilation which takes place. I had naively assumed that the pathologist would just consider the site of the operation. The language is clinical and your loved one is reduced to nothing more than a cadaver. I decided that no other member of the family would read this report.

There was nothing to do now but wait for the statements from Walsgrave Hospital and life was very difficult. I could not sleep or eat and I felt in a state of despair. I just could not believe that Colin was actually dead. My children, Sarah and my friends were very supportive and very concerned. They all suggested that I go away for a few days to try to regain some energy prior to the Inquest.

My friend Ann and I went for a 7 day cruise to Madeira, Morocco and the Canary Islands. She was very kind and supportive and although it was lovely to get out of the house, it was also very difficult. It was full of couples and this had the affect of making me feel my loss more sharply. One day we were sitting in the square in Marrakesh having a drink and watching all the local hawkers plying their trades. I felt overwhelmed because Colin would have loved all the colour and culture and it hit me like a sledgehammer that he would never be able to enjoy any of these sights again! I dissolved in tears of hopelessness.

I sat on the coach back to ship and felt desolate. I told Ann that I did not think that I could continue with the fight against the hospital because I just did not have the emotional strength. She was kindness itself and said that I did not have to make any decisions at the moment and to just try to enjoy the cruise and see it as an opportunity to regain some strength. She also said that if I wanted to withdraw from the whole thing that was fine too and that it was important to protect myself by not feeling under so much pressure.

I had virtually made the decision to get the Inquest over and done with and then leave it at that, when a strange thing happened. We arrived back at the ship and decided to go for a pre-dinner drink in the piano bar. As I walked in, the pianist looked directly at me and went over to the piano and then began to play "Unforgettable" by Nat King Cole. This was the song played at Colin's funeral and the first tape he ever bought me and I just knew in that moment I had to keep fighting. I knew it was a message from him to carry on.

When we arrived home, the Coroner's Officer advised me that she had exchanged our statements with those of the hospital staff and she said I could call and collect them. As I read them I became incandescent with rage. There was a statement from the Consultant, Daniel Higman, which stated that Colin had made a satisfactory recovery from the first operation, which contradicted the post mortem findings and bore no relation to the reality we had all witnessed. He also stated that he had had little contact with Colin. A Senior House Officer, who also said he had little contact with Colin, other than undertaking the initial admissions procedure, also wrote a statement. Why send statements from those who had had little contact with Colin, it did not make any sense to me? Dr Agaba, who I felt was a major player in Colin's treatment, submitted a statement which was nothing more than a list of bullet points, and this had the effect of making me feel he was being unduly careful about committing pen to paper. Mr Wong submitted a statement but there was no mention of the facts he had disclosed post operatively. There were no statements from the nursing staff.

As I read these statements I was outraged. I was more concerned about what they did not say than what they did, to me they appeared sanitized. I could not comprehend why there were no statements from the nursing staff that had Colin in their care 24/7. I telephoned the Coroner's Officer and made her aware of my concerns and asked whether they could obtain statements from nursing staff and call them as witnesses. She advised me that it was not usual practice to call the nurses. I insisted that I felt they needed to be called if a true picture of what happened to Colin was to emerge, and after all had she not told me that an Inquest is a fact finding exercise? It was my belief that had the nurses recorded their notes accurately and passed the correct information on to the doctors, Colin's condition may have become apparent. The Coroner's Officer said she would discuss it with the Coroner and get back to me. She did this and phoned me later in the day to say that the Coroner had agreed to ask for the statements and call two of the nurses as witnesses. I was relieved and grateful to the Coroner.

During this conversation, the Coroner's Officer told me that the Legal Department at Walsgrave Hospital had seen ours statements and now wished to resubmit or amend some of theirs! I was incredulous. How could this be right? It then occurred to me that when they wrote their statements, they were unaware of what information I had but now they knew, they wanted to change theirs! I became upset and relayed this to the Coroner's Officer who reminded me that it was in my interests to get all the information from them and this was a fact finding exercise for The Coroner. Even though this made sense, I was not convinced. I am a lay person and to me, the truth is the truth, and you do not need a practice run first!

During our conversation, The Coroner's Officer dropped another bomb-shell when she told me that the Trust had appointed a Barrister to represent them. I could not understand this. I had been told that an Inquest is a non-adversarial hearing, so I asked myself why they thought they needed a Barrister.

At this stage I realised that I was dealing with more than Colin's death. I was dealing with the weight of a huge bureaucratic organisation which would not admit mistakes and welcome the truth easily. Up until this point I had considered that I was the best person to represent the family at the Inquest because I had been with Colin throughout and I knew first hand what had happened to him. However, when I heard The Trust had appointed a Barrister I felt very concerned. Whilst I had no problem representing myself, I reckoned that I was no match for an experienced Barrister. At this point I felt that perhaps I should consult a solicitor. I did not want to because I could almost hear Colin saying they were all sharks. I did not want to escalate things but I wanted answers and an apology but I felt the Trust was forcing my hand. There was no other option. If they wanted a fight, well I would have to be a formidable contender.

I spoke to my boss Ron Watkins. He had a friend who was a solicitor and he took me to see him. I told him what had happened and he said that he would be happy to represent me at the Inquest. I asked him lots of questions and although he was a really pleasant man and I presume an excellent solicitor, I did not want to hand Colin over to him! It was just something I felt strongly - a gut reaction. My friend Ann then spotted an advertisement for a local legal firm which specialised in medical negligence cases. She telephoned and made an appointment for us both to go along to discuss the situation. Before five minutes had passed, I knew I did not want this man to represent Colin's interests. He was brash and showed off throughout the interview and I knew Colin would not like him.

I had come to the conclusion that I would just have to face the Barrister myself, when some-one within the hospital gave me a piece of paper with the telephone number of a firm of Birmingham Solicitors, Irwin Mitchell, who specialised in medical negligence. I was reluctant because I did not want to go to litigation; I just wanted answers and an apology. Ann said it would do no harm to speak to them and then make a decision. With Ann by my side, I telephoned Irwin Mitchell and was put through to a woman who was gentle and kind. She asked me a few questions and I could hardly speak between sobs. Her patience was endless and when she had gleaned all the information she needed she explained what would happen next. She told me that she would take the information to her team and they would decide whether they would be able to represent me. She explained that they only considered those cases which they felt had a good chance of being successful.

The Team would meet later in the week and following that meeting she would contact me, however, she phoned later that day saying they had already discussed it and offered me an appointment later that week.

I went to Birmingham armed with all the notes I had obtained from the hospital and the Coroner's Office and I was convinced that this meeting would be as fruitless as the previous two. I could not have been more wrong. I met a solicitor called Jonathan Peacock and within minutes of meeting him, I knew he was a safe pair of hands into which I could entrust Colin. He was quietly spoken, warm, gentle, thoughtful and professional. He seemed very knowledgeable and I just knew that he believed me when I told him what had happened to Colin and that he would do his very best to prove it. Jonathon asked me what outcome I was hoping for and I told him that this was not about money but I wanted three things. I wanted to know exactly what had happened to Colin, an apology and assurances about what steps would be put in place to ensure that this could not happen to another human being. He agreed that he would represent the family at the Inquest, would start gathering information and would be in touch with me shortly. I left his office and as I sat on the train, I knew this was a decision Colin would approve of – even though Jonathon was a solicitor! I also felt that I could share the load at last.

Now that legal representation for the Inquest was arranged, I turned my attention to other aspects. I contacted the Coroner and asked him if he would agree to an independent Consultant examining Colin's case. He said that he would and that he would consider who he felt to be the most appropriate person to approach and he would let me know when he had arranged this.

One other thing was causing me great concern. I had read Mr Wong's statement for the Coroner and it did not include some of the information and photographs he had shown me at Colin's post operative meeting. I felt that I needed to speak to him. I phoned his secretary and made an appointment to see him.

I attended the meeting with my friend Mary the following week and it was an emotional one. It was the first time I had seen Mr Wong since Colin's death. He was empathetic and sensitive and expressed his deep sorrow about what had happened to Colin. I told Mr Wong that I had felt compelled to see him because I had to look him in the eye and ask him if he intended to tell the truth at the Inquest and that I needed to ask him some questions. I asked him directly if Colin's condition had been misdiagnosed when he was initially admitted to hospital and he confirmed that it had. Mary asked Mr Wong why no scan had been done prior to operating and Mr Wong explained that this would not have shown the problem. However, he said that a barium enema would and this should have been undertaken. Mary also pointed out that according to the Nursing care plan Colin had had seven bowel movements in two days.

Mr Wong replied:
"How could he, his bowel was blocked with a tumour?"
I said that I had read some of the statements and they bore no relation to what I believed had happened to Colin. I went on to explain that post operatively he had shared photographs and information with me which were not included in his statement. He assured me that he would truthfully answer any questions which were put to him at the Inquest as he would be under oath and that whilst his statement was brief hospital records were available to the Coroner. I knew that Mr Wong was an honourable man and was pleased that I had spoken to him. I knew he was one of the few people within the hospital who I could trust.

There was nothing more to do at the moment apart from wait for the Inquest. It was such a difficult time and I felt that I was in a black hole. My social life had ceased as I did not want to be with people. I felt like an empty shell and had nothing to say to anyone unless it was about Colin, but worst of all I just could not comprehend the fact that he would never walk through the door again. I was utterly miserable and I applaud and thank all my friends who stuck with me throughout because I could not have been easy!
I was advised that the Inquest would go ahead in April and I was relieved as I just wanted it over and done with.

I received a telephone call from the Coroner's Officer one morning in March. She told me that they had been unable to find Dr Agaba. I was confused and asked her what she meant. She then told me that he had left Walsgrave Hospital and no-one knew where he was. I just could not believe what I was hearing. I asked what she was going to do about it, and she said that if he was still in this country she would probably be able to trace him, but if he gone abroad well that was that! I questioned what would happen about the Inquest and she responded by saying that another doctor would have to appear on his behalf. I cried all day because I knew how important it was for Dr Agaba to appear. At about 4.30 p.m. the Coroner's Officer telephoned me and in a bright, jolly voice told me that she had found Mr Agaba working only ten miles away in Warwick. I just could not believe the insensitivity of the woman, and why she could not have checked her facts before raising my anxieties so pointlessly. I think that when dealing with the bereaved it is so important to understand the sensitivity of your role.

In April, I had a telephone call from my friend Merv Samuel, during which he invited me to his 50th Birthday Party on the 23rd April. He was very kind and said that he would understand if I could not face it but he hoped that I would come. After talking to Kate and Gill, both persuaded me that I should make the effort and Gill said she would come with me and that if at any time, I felt I could not handle things we would leave. Also Kate said she and John would come and collect us. I worked with Merv and knew that lots of friends and colleagues would be there and as I had not yet returned to work, I felt it would be a way of breaking the ice.

So I went on my first social event since Colin's death. People were kindness itself and everyone came over to speak to me, hug me or bring me a glass of wine! I got very upset and so did some of my colleagues. It was good to know that people were supportive and I even had a dance which I would not have believed possible before I left home. I also got very drunk! Each time someone handed me a glass of red wine – I drank it! I do not actually know what I drank but suffice it to say I spent the following two days in bed vomiting copiously and nursing a hang-over of monumental proportions.

A couple of months before Colin died; I was invited together with some of my staff to an "Evening of colour" at a local hotel. It involved a local medium exploring auras etc. It was just a lark as far as I was concerned as I was a sceptic but I thought it would be fun and entertaining.

During the course of the evening, the medium suddenly turned to me and said,
"The lady in the blue suit! I have a message for you."

I was so shocked. My father had recently died and he went on to describe him exactly and then he told me some things that not even my friends knew which convinced me my dad was there. He then went on to say that I should wear amethysts as they would protect me. I was really taken by the things he had told me and rushed home to tell Colin about the message from my dad, and that I was certain he was in touch with him. Colin laughed his socks off and said that he found it difficult to understand how such an intelligent woman could be taken in. He expressed the view that all mediums were charlatans. However, the next evening when we were eating our meal, he slid a little box across the table. Inside was a pair of antique amethyst ear-rings. I asked him what they were for and said I thought he did not believe the mumbo jumbo. He told me that he was 99% certain it was rubbish but because of the 1% the ear-rings were my insurance policy!

A couple of weeks after Merv's party, my friend Mary said that she had been invited to a friend's house and that the medium that had been at the hotel was there. I could not see him because there were only five slots which were all taken, but I said I would go to keep her company. When we arrived, she said that it was me who was going to see him. I went into him with very mixed feelings. I was a sceptic and Colin thought all mediums were charlatans. What was I doing?

No-one in that house nor the medium himself knew me or anything about me. He began by saying that he had Colin there and he was laughing about the red wine and that it was good to see me dancing again!

The medium said,

"Colin says he loves the rose, does that mean anything to you?"

Of course it did, I had just chosen Colin's headstone and had a rose etched onto it, because Colin loved roses and often bought them for me.

He went on, "Tell Colin's daughter he has got his dog back."

I had no idea what that meant but when I phoned Sarah later she told me that the dog her father had given her had died.

There were a lot more things he said to me but I was really taken aback when he said, "Colin says why aren't you wearing the amethyst ear-rings?"

I was so shocked!

As I was leaving the medium said

"There is just one more thing; I don't know if this means anything to you, but Colin says don't give up, justice will prevail."

I just knew that was from Colin because that is a phrase he would have used. I don't know whether I believe or not, but I knew that was Colin talking and I knew that whatever happened at the Inquest I would not stop fighting until Justice had prevailed!

Well the Inquest did not take place as initially planned in April or May because the Coroner's Officer advised me that the hospital could not be ready by then and she said she would set another date in June. That never happened, and at this point the Coroner's Officer advised me that the Coroner was losing patience and if he did not receive the outstanding statements from Walsgrave Hospital he would order a pre-meeting. Following this, the statements were sent from the hospital and a date set for 1st and 2nd August for the Inquest. All of this had a negative effect on all the family because you prepare yourself psychologically for the event and work up towards the date, only to be shattered when it is cancelled repeatedly. The process is an emotional roller coaster and not an easy one to survive.

Whilst I appreciate that hospitals are very busy places and doctors need to concern themselves with the living, there is very little compassion for those who have died and those who are grieving. Indeed the grief is compounded by their inconsiderate behaviour which is particularly galling when you feel that their actions have contributed to the death of the person you loved.

CHAPTER 8
THE INQUEST

At last after four false starts the Inquest went ahead on the 1st August. It had seemed an endless wait but now we believed we would get the answers we so needed and we would witness justice being done. Friends and family met at my house and we went together to the Courts. I was relieved that I had all their support because when we arrived, we were besieged by television cameras and the press, all wanting statements or interviews.

When we got inside the Court, it was a very difficult experience for everyone. We sat in a waiting area alongside those who were appearing before Magistrates for Criminal Offences, several of whom were shouting, swearing and having heated discussions with their lawyers. For those of us unused to frequenting the Courts, it was not a happy situation!

In the same waiting area, the hospital staff and witnesses also appeared with their Barrister. She was clearly briefing them on their statements and evidence as they huddled

closely around her. It was very painful for me to have to sit alongside the people I held responsible for Colin's death. Mr Agaba said hello to me, but I was unable to even acknowledge him.
I felt angry and heartbroken.

The process was that the hospital staff would give evidence on the first day and the family would give evidence on the second day. The Jury was sworn in and the legal arguments put forward and then the Inquest began. As each witness gave their evidence, it soon became clear Colin had not received the level of care he should have expected and that he had been misdiagnosed prior to the first operation.

The Expert Witness, Dr Agaba and Mr Higman gave evidence in the morning followed by the nurses in the afternoon.

The language throughout contained legal and medical jargon but what we learned was that Mr Agaba's initial working diagnosis was wrong and that all further problems stemmed from this. The Expert Witness called by the Coroner concluded from the operation notes that, "the operative findings are not consistent with the earlier diagnosis of bowel obstruction. Indeed part of the bowel was there to be seen in Theatre." It appears that Dr Agaba had initially thought that the bowel was involved, but his operation notes stated that there was no bowel involved, but instead of reappraising his earlier diagnosis, he stitched Colin back up without further analysis.

We had always known in our hearts that this was the cause of Colin's problems and subsequent death, but no-one had taken the time or trouble to explain and apologise to us. The culture within the hospital had ensured that the only way we would find out was via an Inquest.

The Coroner pointed out that, "Mr Agaba noted that the bowel was unaffected by what he had done and he wrote this down. It therefore follows that after the operation Mr Agaba knew or should have known that he had not removed the obstruction in Mr Meaney's colon and yet it seems no action was taken. There was not, according to the evidence any further diagnostic enquiry as to the cause of the obstruction. Perhaps a scan or x-ray. Perhaps even a stool record count. Mr Agaba reported the outcome of the operation to Mr Higman, his Senior Consultant. Had he reported as fully as he did in the records, Mr Higman might have realised all was not well."

Mr Higman took to the stand and I was struck by his arrogance, but what really shocked me was the fact when the Coroner questioned him about the fact that according to hospital records he had said that Colin was taking fluids and diet normally and passing stools; he suggested that some patients tell nurses they are eating etc and that perhaps Colin had done so. I was so outraged; I had to leave the Court room. What kind of a man is it who blames the victim?

The Coroner summed up Mr Higman's role:
"Mr Meaney was returned to the Ward. He was seen by Mr Higman's Registrar the following day. She reported to Mr Higman that Mr Meaney felt nauseated and had no bowel action even to passing wind. That of course would be right. His bowel or colon was still blocked or substantially blocked by the cancer according to both Mr Wong and Mr Everson (consultant in general and colorectal surgery,

Leicester Royal Infirmary – appointed by the coroner to provide an independent medical report). Mr Higman saw him on the 21st December and it was reported to him that 3 days after the operation Mr Meaney was not eating and nauseous and Mr Higman felt the patient to be suffering from ileus. Mr Higman says the plan was to allow Mr Meaney home if the symptoms resolved. Indeed the Registrar discharged him home on 24th December and according to the family sick, not eating and as we now know with a cancer blocking his colon or bowel. According to the hospital records however, "eating and drinking and going to the toilet."

Mr Wong was next to give evidence and as far as I am concerned, he is the only member of staff from Walsgrave Hospital to emerge from the Inquest with decency, honesty and integrity. He explained what had happened to Colin and answered all the questions put to him in a forthright manner.

The Coroner noted, "Mr Wong gave evidence that on the 27th December, when Mr Meaney had had to wait in such dreadful conditions that do the hospital no credit; on the other side of the fence Mr Wong had 50 patients to deal with and had no assistance from any other Consultant. He had been on duty for several days and it was clear from what he said that he was angry. He even asked Mr Agaba to contact Mr Higman but to no avail. He stayed on during what was to be his holiday break. It is worth noting that the Independent Pathologist found no fault with Mr Wong's surgery."

Where was Mr Higman? He was after all, the Consultant in charge of Colin's care. Was he contactable and if not why not? These are questions which were not answered at the Inquest and have never been answered elsewhere.

In the afternoon, it was the nurses turn to give evidence and I was so glad that I had asked the Coroner to put them on the stand. I had felt so strongly that they had allowed Colin's distress to continue, and that if they had reported effectively to doctors, things may have been so different. Their evidence confirmed all my feelings. Their nursing notes showed a completely different picture from the one I had witnessed, and more worryingly the notes were out of sequence and so appeared to have been recorded retrospectively.

The Coroner noted, "Let's look at the evidence that he was eating drinking and opening his bowels. Sister Wilson was quite clear on 21st December Mr Meaney was not tolerating fluids and still vomiting and intravenous fluids were recommenced. She said on 22nd December he opened his bowels three times. Indeed in nursing records there is some evidence of him passing a small stool. Yet we know he could have passed little or nothing for his colon was blocked. The following day she said he began diet. An interesting word. I note she did not use the words ate or food or meal – and why – such words could hardly be used to describe a spoon or so of mashed up cornflakes. Yet the lack of use of plain English misled the discharging doctor."

The nurses who took the stand were not impressive and floundered when asked questions. In my opinion it was clear for all to see that their evidence was not reliable based on the information we had already heard.

I appreciate that medical and nursing staff are busy and need to return to their posts quickly, but I felt overwhelmingly that they should be forced to remain at the Inquest long enough to hear the evidence of the family. It would benefit them greatly to witness first hand the emotional turmoil and pain of bereaved families and it may impact on their practice.

After the first day, we spoke to Jonathan Peacock our solicitor, about the proceedings and he advised that all was going as expected and important details were emerging. He reassured us about the following day when we had to give our evidence. I had mixed feelings about this. On the one hand I was so relieved that the day had arrived when I could go on the stand and tell the world what Walsgrave had done to Colin but on the other I was anxious that I would not do him justice.

In the event, I can honestly say that all of us did Colin proud. I gave my evidence first and I knew Colin was standing beside me as I told his story. Mary went next and she made it quite clear what she thought of the nurse's evidence and being a nurse she was well qualified to do so. She pointed out that the notes were recorded retrospectively and that, "they beggared belief". Brian and John followed and they recounted events about Colin's stay in hospital and subsequent discharge. Their evidence was very powerful. Jonathan summed up and the Jury were directed by the Coroner. He outlined the range of verdicts they could bring in, explaining which were appropriate and which were not in these particular circumstances.

We sat outside the courtroom feeling very anxious. The Coroner had instructed the jury to try to reach a verdict today rather than have us all come back after the weekend. This was important because Sarah, Colin's daughter, was going to France immediately after the hearing, and she so needed this break with her children after the trauma she had endured.

After an anxious wait, we were all called back into Court and the chairman of the Jury told the Coroner that they were finding it difficult to come to a conclusion because although they realised that they should bring in an "Accidental death" verdict due to the legal system, they asked if they could add "through negligence". The Coroner went on to explain that they could not do this and why. He also went to pains to point out that the Coronial system was outdated and under review and that narrative verdicts were being considered. It was apparent that some of the Jurors were visibly upset by this as plainly they wished to bring in a verdict other than "Accidental death". The Coroner went on to explain to the Jury, "that such a verdict does not deprive any person of a civil remedy they might otherwise have had, and it does not exonerate a person implicated in the death from blame."

The Jury retired and came back with an "Accidental Death" verdict but we could see that some members of the Jury were visibly upset.

The Coroner summed up and said that he appreciated that this verdict did not fully reflect what had happened and that there were gross failings on the part of Walsgrave Hospital and that was that! Over!

I felt that not only had Colin been let down by the medical system but also the legal system. I was so upset. I spoke to Jonathan who said that the press were waiting outside the Court and that we needed to make a statement. I asked him to do this on behalf of the family. He said that what he had heard in Court convinced him that we should make a complaint to the General Medical Council about Mr Higman and Dr Agaba who were involved in Colin's lack of care.

We all walked outside to be greeted by television cameras and reporters, and Jonathan made a statement on behalf of the family and stated that we would be reporting the doctors to the GMC. I noticed that the Chairman of the Trust was also speaking to the TV cameras. When I got home, I switched on the television to hear what he was saying. I was incredulous to hear him say that the Trust does not accept what the Coroner had said and they would be considering their position. I was taken aback by the arrogance of that statement and although I felt devastated I knew I would make him eat those words. This was Colin we were dealing with.

The following day all the local papers and some Nationals carried the story and The Birmingham Post August 3rd 2002 reported as follows:

"Hospital "failed" cancer patient.
A Midland Coroner yesterday attacked laws which barred an inquest from finding a hospital negligent after it failed to spot that a patient had cancer early enough to save him.
City Coroner David Sarginson condemned the hospital for "gross failings" in its care of the 64 year old, of Daventry Road, Coventry. He also rounded on the current laws governing inquests, which are under review.
After the Jury returned a verdict of accidental death on Mr Meaney, Mr Sarginson said the result did not "fully reflect" the shortcomings of the hospital.

He explained to the Hearing at Coventry Magistrates Court that under current legislation, the jury was not allowed to find the hospital negligent because two experts had said on oath that there was no conclusive link between the delay in its diagnosis of the cancer and Mr Meaney's death.

Mr Sarginson said: "I fully appreciate this verdict does not reflect fully what happened. We are stuck with the old system, it is not what we need in the 21st Century.

Outside the Court Mr Meaney's family, including his partner Kathleen Lee said they would sue the hospital and take the matter to the General Medical Council.

Family Solicitor Johnathan Peacock said "The inquest today identified gross failings in the work of two surgeons. The family are determined that lessons will be learned from this tragedy. Legal action will be pursued and the matter will go to the General Medical Council."

Earlier the inquest heard how Mr Meaney was admitted to the Walsgrave Hospital on December 18th last year after his GP thought he had a hernia problem.

Mr Sarginson said that the surgeon who operated on Mr Meaney, Dr Emanuel Agaba, should have spotted the cancerous tumour but failed to do so.

The mistake was compounded by the chain of nursing staff, who eventually discharged Mr Meaney on Christmas Eve, only for him to be readmitted three days later in agony. A second operation discovered the cancer in the colon, but Mr Meaney died on January 11. Mr Sarginson said "There was a gross failure to procure medical provision for this patient in hospital, Dr Agaba's working diagnosis was incorrect. I would venture to say to you that that is gross failure."

After the hearing a spokesman for Walsgrave hospital said there were no plans to conduct an inquiry into the surgeons' performance."

I read the article and was pleased that it summed up the situation but when I read the last paragraph, I was speechless. Whilst I was beginning to get the measure of the Trust, to the point where little surprised me, I still found it difficult to believe that a spokesman could have sat through the inquest and then made a public statement such as this. What hope was there! That statement just fed my desire to force them to make a public apology to Colin.

CHAPTER 9
WHAT NOW?

Following the Inquest, things felt very dark. I felt that justice certainly had not been done but was unsure what I should do next. I was in such a distressed state, it was impossible to think clearly. I just do not know how I would have survived without family and friends. They were with me all the way, and it is so true that in times of crisis you really do find out who your genuine friends are, and I was so blessed with mine.

Mary and Pete were wonderful. They insisted I came to them anytime night or day and they made sure I ate. Veronica, my friend, would speak to me on the phone during the day and if she sensed I was despairing she would just turn up after work with an over- night bag and stay with me. She had such understanding for one so young. Gill would turn up and take me out and attend meetings with me. There was Ann who would talk to me day and night and just knew when I needed support. Sarah, Colin's daughter, would drive down from Derbyshire with her two small children and stay for weekends in spite of the fact she was greatly suffering the loss of the father she loved so much. Then of course there was my family. Kate and John were amazing. They took me on holiday and just turned up night and day to support me. Kate always knew how I was feeling, she never had to ask. Mat appeared to do whatever jobs needed doing around the house, I never had to ask him, he just knew. Andy, my nephew, was some-one who offered emotional and practical support whenever I needed it along with his parents, Brian and Val. I truly came to learn that angels are not in Heaven, they are here on earth alongside you when you need them most. In spite of this support I still needed some direction.

I asked Colin to help me find a way forward and I remembered that when I used to get angry or upset about some injustice or other, he would quietly say,

"Don't get mad, get even."

That thought spurred me on. I remember that on the day following the Inquest I got out of bed at 3.00 a.m. and decided to write to the Coroner. I told him that Colin had been badly let down by the Coronial system and asked why a Jury is appointed if they are not able to return the verdict they feel is right and proper? I also asked him how I might have some input into the Commission reviewing the law into Inquests.

The Coroner wrote to me by return. His letter was sympathetic and informative. He urged me to write to Tom Luce, the Chairman of the Coroners' Fundamental Review, to give my opinions. I have nothing but praise for the Coroner, Mr Sarginson. I was to speak to him on several occasions over the next few months and he was supportive and helpful. He told me that if I supplied seven tapes to the

Coroners' Officer, I could have the recording of the Inquest.

A few days later I wrote to the Coroners' Fundamental Review, outlining the facts of Colin's case and the outcome of the Inquest. I told them that I felt an overwhelming sense of injustice which was compounded by events at the Inquest. A few days later I received a telephone call from a gentleman who was dealing with the Review, and he said that he had been very moved by my letter and he asked me to come to London to speak to the review. Of course, I agreed to go. A few days later I received a letter asking me to read and comment on the consultation document and to bring my comments to London. I spoke to the Committee in September. I read the consultation paper and I could see so much that needed to change if the Coronial system was going to improve. I wrote five pages outlining what changes I felt should take place. This is something I would never have been able to do prior to the events surrounding Colin's death. Experience is most certainly the best teacher! This is why it is so important for those who have such experiences to try to find the strength to bring them into the open and pass them on to others.

I went to London on the 26th September with my dear friend Ann, and although I felt quite anxious I spoke to the Committee and told them what changes I felt should happen. They told me they were thankful and moved by my words, but even more gratifying was the fact that I received a letter the following March, thanking me for my submissions and asking if I would mind being included on a list of contributors which would appear in the published report. I was elated because this was the first indication to me that perhaps Colin's death had not been quite so pointless! If the law was going to be changed, he was contributing to this and just as importantly, someone was listening.

I held the letter up to Colin's photograph and said, "this one is for you Colin."

I now had to ensure there would be more!
A few days after my trip to London I received a telephone call from the Coroners' Officer to advise me that the tapes were ready for collection. I was relieved because after much consideration I had decided to submit a complaint to the GMC, and obviously I wanted to be sure that the information stored in my head was accurate. I knew it was going to be painful to listen to them but told myself to get on with it and submit the complaint. I put the first tape in and although the quality was not good, I could hear the proceedings. Then suddenly, the tape became blank. I assumed that there must be something wrong with my recorder. I fiddled with the knobs and the volume but to no avail. I thought there must be a faulty tape and so I put the second tape in but still there was nothing. All seven tapes proved to be blank. I was in turmoil. I just could not believe it. I phoned the Coroners' Officer and was told that the system had malfunctioned and not recorded and nothing could be done. I felt so angry and asked whether anyone had thought to check the tapes before sending them to me, or had they not checked the system was working in the Court. I was so distressed and worried. I needed that information for my complaint. I wrote to the Coroner and he telephoned me to say that I could have a copy of his own hand written transcript. I was so grateful and appreciative of his wonderful support.

In the month's following the Inquest, life became very difficult and at times I felt despairing that I would ever move forward. I had to prepare the papers for the GMC complaint, and again, the Coroner was very helpful, supplying me with some hand-written papers and Jonathan Peacock also provided me with information to forward to them. Jonathan also submitted his own report. I completed all the paper-work and knew nothing would happen for some time. I went with Ann to London, and personally handed the whole file and paperwork in to the GMC as I felt unable to trust them in the post.

Just after returning from London, I was slowly, pointlessly, meandering around the Tesco store which is near to the Walsgrave hospital. It was late afternoon and the reality was that it was a cold, dark, dismal day, and I was trying to avoid returning to a cold miserable empty house. I always found the weekend the most difficult time. Colin and I had always loved Friday night when work was over for the week and he would buy me flowers and get some good wine, and we would have a special meal in or go out to eat. I felt so unhappy as I walked around the store when suddenly I spotted Mr Higman, the Consultant, wheeling his trolley past me. My heart lurched as I recognised him from the Inquest, but what really hurt was that in his trolley I saw flowers and wine. I felt sick as I realised nothing had changed in his life whilst mine felt as though it was over. I felt violent and had an overwhelming urge to hit him. I took some deep breaths, left my trolley and walked out of the store. I sat in my car hardly able to breathe, but when I calmed down all I could think about was how glad I was that I had made that trip to London to the GMC.

The first Christmas following Colin's death was fast approaching and the prospect threw me in to turmoil. I did not know how I was going to get through it. Colin had loved Christmas, and the thought that he would not be with me this Christmas was so painful. After talking to my family I decided that I did not want to be at home. This was a difficult decision as I had never been apart from my family ever at Christmas time. I had spent every Christmas with my mum since I was born but Christmas now had such painful negative memories. Colin was discharged from hospital on Christmas Eve and suffered so much over Christmas Day and Boxing Day, and then he went onto a life support machine on New Year's Eve. I just felt that I had to be away from all the jollity and celebrations and did not want to spoil them for everybody else. I believed that if I removed myself from the scene of Colin's distress then it would somehow be easier to bear, and that if the family did not see me, then perhaps they could also forget and enjoy themselves for a short time.

In the event I went with my friend, Ann, to Venice. We chose Venice because we felt that it would probably be less Christmassy because of the all the international visitors, and we were right. My son, Matthew, found us a beautiful hotel just around the corner from St Mark's Square, and it proved to be the right decision for me. Everything was open and we decided that we would do the tourist bit on Christmas Day visiting all the famous sites. There was only one problem! On Christmas Day we went to breakfast and I took what I thought was my blood pressure tablet only to find that I had mistakenly taken a sleeping tablet! Poor Ann had to do the tourist bit alone as I slept off the effects of the tablet.

However, by lunchtime I had surfaced and we went for a non-Christmas lunch of seafood.

When I returned home I found that my mum had been admitted to hospital and I had to go straight from the airport to her bedside. This was not what I had planned, and I found it really difficult to return to that same hospital, a year after Colin had been there and, of course, the images flooded my mind.

After Christmas I began to feel very unwell and experienced chest pain and arrhythmia.
I felt the need to get back to my job and went into work, but I just sat in my office crying for the whole day, and was unable to engage with people or the job. I tried again a few days later but suffered the same experience. I felt an abject failure and that my life as I had known it was in tatters. My employer was very understanding and told me to take as long as I needed and not to put myself under any more pressure. As the manager of a team, I was conscious that my absence was putting everyone else under pressure and so the stress was a vicious circle.

I eventually went to my GP who listened to my heart and referred me to a heart Consultant. He did an ECG and said it had shown some abnormalities and suggested I wear a monitor for twenty four hours as this would give an indication of what was happening as far as my heart was concerned.

This monitor showed abnormalities and the Consultant suggested a heart scan. At the time, I was not remotely concerned. I just did not care if I lived or died. Fortunately, the heart scan showed nothing significant and the Consultant said he felt the problem was due to the bereavement and all the pressures surrounding it. I also suffered several severe attacks of a colon problem, my blood pressure was very high, and I became an insomniac. The situation was taking its toll on my previous good health. I was permanently concerned that I was absent from work but knew I was in no fit state to do my job. As the manager of a counselling service, essential to my work was the need to be emotionally resilient and contain the anxiety and sadness of others. How could I do this when I felt so bereft?

My boss visited several times and he said that if I felt unable to return to work the possibility of early retirement was available. He stressed that it was my decision and the job was there if I felt able to return but he suggested I consider the other option and that just knowing it was available might take the pressure off me.

This threw me into further confusion. My state of mind at that time meant that decision making was a near impossibility! I spoke to my children Kate and Matt about it and they felt I should retire because neither could see me returning to a job that entailed dealing with people who themselves were experiencing trauma. I was worried that I would not cope financially and psychologically, as I had a small pension and I had always loved my work, but I knew that I had little left to offer clients and staff, and so I made the decision to take up the offer of early retirement and I finished exactly one year after Colin's death in January 2003.

The following months were hard to bear because Jonathan Peacock was preparing a case against Walsgrave Hospital, and there were lots of letters back and forth and telephone conversations between us. One letter contained a report from a Professor of Surgery, which confirmed all that Colin had been through. In May, Jonathan advised me that he was sending a letter to Walsgrave Hospital making a claim against them, and that they had three months in which to reply. I seemed to be permanently waiting for something to happen.

I realised that I had to try to resolve some issues in my life. I needed to sort out my financial issues such as probate and mortgages. At this stage my nephew, Andrew, stepped in and took this over for me. He diligently sorted out everything and took a great weight off my shoulders. He also came with me to some appointments with Jonathan and helped me with some major decisions. My daughter Kate insisted that I start going swimming with her several times a week because she said that if I felt better physically, it would help me recover psychologically. Sarah often came to spend weekends with me, bringing her small children. I then decided that I should get a dog to ease my loneliness and the emptiness within the house. I bought the loveliest little white, fluffy, Tibetan Terrier puppy, who I called Smudge. He has grown into a large white mop of a dog, who adores people, and has untold love to give. He is like a reincarnation of Colin. He has white hair, has a great sense of fun, is very sociable and loveable, he loves people and he is very intelligent. Getting Smudge was such a positive move. Dogs have to be walked every day and it motivated me to go out, and when you are out you meet and interact with people. The house felt less empty and I felt a little less alone. Smudge just seemed to sense when I was at my lowest, and he would climb up and snuggle into me, and when I cried he often climbed up on the sofa and licked the tears from my face.

I then decided that I needed to do something with my time. I was just sitting at home and could think of nothing but what had happened to Colin and the fight I had on my hands. Friends and family were so supportive and visited often, and the advice from most of them was that I really needed to find something to do. But what could I do? I knew that I could certainly not go back to the job I had been doing. I had trained and worked as a social worker for many years, and although I had not done the job in recent years, a colleague suggested that perhaps I could go back into social work a few hours a week via an agency. She brought a card with the details of an agency she knew and told me to phone and speak to a particular person. I kept the card for weeks. I had totally lost all my confidence, I just kept asking myself what anyone would want with a clapped out social worker, because that is exactly how I felt.

One day I told myself that this was the day I had to make that phone call. I forced myself to pick up the phone and speak to some-one in the agency. The woman I spoke to was delightful and asked me to come to Birmingham the following day for an interview. I remember panicking on the train and I almost went back home, but my friend, Ann, was with me and she insisted I had nothing to lose by hearing what they had to say. The interview was very relaxed and all went well as she told me she was impressed by my qualifications, experience and the jobs I had held. She then asked me why I had left my last job. As I began to explain to her I broke down and sobbed, and within minutes she was sobbing too! We dried our tears and had a cup of tea. Thank goodness, in spite of the tears, she believed in my ability and within a couple of days she telephoned me to offer me several placements, and said that all were prepared to let me work a couple of days a week. One of the placements was at Walsgrave Hospital! My children told me not to go near the place, but in a bizarre way I felt really drawn to it. I spoke to the Manager, and she agreed I could work two days a week, and the placement would last 3 months. I felt that this would provide me with an opportunity to see whether I could manage to work again and provide the service that clients deserved.

I remember well, the morning I was due to start work. I was so anxious and afraid I would not cope. I had not been in social work for several years and I felt a shell of the person I had once been. I was shown into an office which I would share with Dot, Andrea and later Safina and Edwina, and they were kindness itself. There were difficult times with the GMC and the case against the hospital but they were one hundred percent supportive and helped me through it all the way. There is no doubt that their support and love aided my recovery and I am eternally grateful because I realise it could have been so different if I had gone to another team. I ended up staying there for three years. Around this time, I also felt that I needed to do something about what was happening within the NHS and although not at my best intellectually, I applied to be an auditor with The Healthcare Commission (then CHI) visiting hospitals. No-one was more surprised than me when I got the job. I only did two audits because after taking part, I realised that it was too soon for me to take part in such an undertaking, and so I stopped. I was also not convinced about the audits because at that time it was not possible to ask patients what they felt, and that seemed very odd because whatever service you are reviewing, my view is that the person who uses the service is exactly the person who should be asked!

CHAPTER 10
THE ROAD TO JUSTICE

There is little doubt that going to work, even for two days a week was making a difference to my life. It provided some routine and sense of purpose. I began to regain some of my confidence and in spite of everything I found myself laughing again. I still felt driven to find answers but more confident in my search. I had a growing sense of frustration that I had heard nothing from the hospital. I had stupidly thought that when the inquest was over some-one from the hospital might have got in touch and explained what had gone wrong and might even say, "We are sorry".

Of course, nothing happened and I felt aggrieved that no one cared. I decided to take matters into hand and so at the beginning of June I wrote a letter to David Roberts, the Chief Executive of the Trust, asking him the questions to which I wanted answers. Three weeks later, I still had not received a reply so I telephoned his office and his secretary told me that there was a letter on his desk waiting to be signed and I would receive this the following day. When it had not arrived days later, I decided I would take more positive action. As I was working in the next building to the Chief Executive, I saw that he came to work very early in the morning and so I went into work very early one morning and telephoned his office and I asked to speak to David as though it were a personal call. No-one was more surprised than me when I was put straight through to him, although I think I detected surprise in his voice! He apologised and said the letter was still on his desk and that he had not signed it. At this point I told him I did not want a letter, I wanted to meet him personally and discuss the issues. He was extremely pleasant and agreed to a meeting which took place on the 9th July. The letter arrived a day prior to the meeting. I was surprised that he apologised unreservedly for errors regarding Colin's treatment, but I still needed to know that this would not happen again.

I prepared for this meeting because I wanted him to take it seriously and to try to encourage his understanding of the importance of dealing properly with the death of a person in these circumstances. I took several photographs of Colin to that meeting so that he could see that we were talking about a beloved partner, father, grandfather and friend and not just a statistic and the meeting lasted one and a half hours.

He was patient and he heard my story and told me it was the most lucid, moving account he had heard and it was clear that I had all the facts. He said he had not been in his post when these things happened to Colin, and that he did not wish to be part of an organisation that treated people in such a manner, and went on to say that he was not sure what action he would take at the moment, and he needed time to think things through. Mr Roberts continued that he intended to audit nursing on the ward and apologised sincerely about what had happened to Colin, and asked me

what he could do to give me some closure. I said that I needed to be able to say to Colin, "I'm sorry I couldn't stop them killing you but I've made sure that they put things right so that no-one else dies needlessly."
I told him that I did not wish to receive glib letters stating that lessons had been learned; I wanted evidence that changes had been put into place. Mr Roberts was reassuring and told me he wanted to say sorry to Colin and that it may take time but he would do this. He said that he accepted that Walsgrave Hospital had not given me many reasons to trust it, but he asked me to trust him. I said I would, and that he had better not let me down because if he did I would not disappear into the ether. He actually gave me a hug when I was leaving and I really hoped he was genuine and that this was a man I could trust.

On leaving he said that he would look into all my queries and would start a process of change, and that he would keep in touch with me and let me know when he had more information.

I waited three months for a telephone call and when one was not forthcoming, I telephoned him and reminded him that he said he would be in touch with me and that I had heard nothing. He told me that as I was taking legal action against the hospital he could not speak to me. So much for effective communication and the learning of lessons!

Following the Inquest, Jonathan Peacock had written to two Coventry Members of Parliament expressing concern about the lack of care Colin had received and advising them that he had two similar cases from the same hospital, both of whom had fortunately survived. This had prompted the MPs to write to David Roberts, the Chief Executive, outlining their concerns and asking him to explain what had happened to Colin and what would be done to put things right for other patients. It must be remembered that the Inquest had taken place and that Mr Roberts had the advantage of having in his possession all the facts which were uncovered at the Inquest, prior to responding to the MPs. However, he just regurgitated all the statements that had been prepared prior to the Inquest.

I asked Mr Roberts why when he had replied to the MP he quoted verbatim from the nursing notes despite the fact that the Coroner had dismissed these as a "wish list". He told me he had not written the letter himself, but that he would look into it. I suggested that perhaps he should do that before signing letters in the future if lessons were really going to be learnt.

Prior to visiting the Chief Executive, I had received the outcome of the General Medical Council enquiry. Throughout the year this had been ongoing and there were many ups and downs along the way. I was sent both doctors' statements to read and to comment on if I wished to do so. They made for difficult reading and opened old wounds. I felt sorry for Dr Agaba and from the tone of his defence I felt that he was truly sorry about what had happened to Colin, and I was always aware that he was the junior doctor in all of this and he should have been supervised more closely.

However, I could not find the same degree of compassion for Mr Higman. Although the letter did say he was sorry for the distress caused to the patient and his family, I felt there was an air of arrogance about his statement, confirmed by the fact that he enclosed his CV listing eight pages of all his research and writings, all of which demonstrated that he is indeed very learned. However, his intellect was not in question here, but rather the poor care and treatment received by Colin. I also felt that as the Consultant and Senior doctor, he had a higher degree of responsibility for Colin's care.

I received a letter from the General Medical Council stating that they had considered my complaint against both doctors and had determined that the case should be referred to the Preliminary Proceedings Committee. I was surprised, but satisfied with this action, because I had believed that the complaint would be thrown out at the first hurdle and it was gratifying to know that I was being heard. I also felt it would make both doctors concerned enough to ensure that they would be more careful in the future and that was all I wanted. I received a letter dated 22nd May 2003 from the General Medical Council, in which they informed me that the Committee concluded that the allegations did not raise an issue of serious professional misconduct, but they made the following comments:

"The Committee were of the view that as Mr Meaney was in Mr Higman's care he should have taken a more proactive role in objectively reviewing the post-operative findings with Dr Agaba, even though Dr Agaba was not on his team, particularly as Mr Meaney's condition failed to improve. The Committee were also concerned by Mr Higman's comments in his observations to the Committee in which he attempted to attribute blame for these shortcomings on others.

The Committee noted that Dr Agaba's view (which formed part of his differential diagnosis) that the obstruction was due to the bowel being entrapped in the hernia and considered this diagnosis, although subsequently proved to be wrong, was reasonable in the circumstances. It noted that Dr Agaba had sought assistance from a Consultant when he encountered difficulties during the course of the second operation.

Notwithstanding the fact that the Committee recognised that there were shortcomings in the standard of care provided to Mr Meaney, it concluded that these allegations did not reach the threshold of serious professional misconduct. Whilst the committee noted the Coroner's findings that there had been "gross failure" in Mr Meaney's care, this failure was not attributed by the Coroner directly to an individual doctor.

Nevertheless, the Committee has asked me to convey its advice to Mr Higman and Dr Agaba. Mr Higman has been reminded of the importance of supervising junior members of staff more effectively and taking a more proactive role in reviewing difficult cases. Dr Agaba has been reminded of his duties as a registered doctor and the standards he has to maintain when treating patients; which would include making an effective diagnosis, taking into account all relevant clinical findings, and to consider differential diagnoses where appropriate. The Committee have also asked me to draw both doctors' attention to Dr Everson's conclusions at pages 3 and 4 of his report dated 1 July 2003, which highlights the importance of listening to patients and their relatives' concerns. Both doctors have been advised to ensure that they follow this guidance in their future practice."

I was satisfied with this outcome. I felt that I had been listened to and that perhaps this referral to the GMC would improve the practice of these doctors in future cases. I felt it would just be a minor dent in their careers whilst providing me with some sense of justice for Colin.

CHAPTER 11
THE END OF THE ROAD

Jonathan Peacock now took over most of the work from me. He was representing me in the action against the hospital and I found this a particularly difficult time although Jonathan was very kind and supportive. There was so much correspondence to deal with as letters went back and forth between Jonathan and the hospital, and between Jonathan and me. This is so difficult for people who are not used to dealing with the legal process and some of the letters are very distressing. If the letter was going to be distressing Jonathan always phoned and warned me it was coming and explained it to me.

From the outset I had always said this action was not about money. How could any amount of money replace a beautiful human being like Colin? However, it is the only means of proving that the hospital was negligent. One morning, I was at home when Jonathan phoned me to tell me that the hospital had made an offer to me. I was surprised because I had been told to expect a protracted length of time before they offered anything. He then told me that the offer was £8000. I was devastated. Not because I wanted money but because I felt that they thought that my precious Colin was worth £8000. I know it is a contradiction because I was not in this for the money, however money is the way in which the NHS demonstrates its culpability and this derisory offer hurt so much. I cried for days. Jonathan explained that they usually started off at a low amount and that I had to see it in legal terms rather than take it personally, and whilst I understood what he meant it felt impossible to do so. This WAS personal, this was Colin.

The following months were hard to bear as numerous letters passed between Jonathan and me. The stack of letters measures about two inches high and each one outlines what the response from the hospital was, or information, or asks questions, but whatever the content, each one was difficult to read and the whole process was a constant source of pain. Throughout the process two incidents really stand out as being horrendously difficult situations to deal with.

The first was when I received a letter and telephone call from one of Jonathan's colleagues. She was very kind and sympathetic and explained to me that she was assisting in making a claim against the hospital and as such she needed so assess the financial loss that had resulted from Colin's death. As a lay person I had no idea what she meant and asked her to explain. She told me that I needed to make a list of all the things that Colin used to do, and that now I had to pay someone to do, and these costs would be added to the claim. For example painting and decorating or gardening. I was heart-broken. I could not believe that I was expected to put a price on the things that Colin had done. I was angry – paying a workman to do the practical tasks was the easy part. How could I put a price on love, companionship, caring, a lost future together, and a lost dream of a happy retirement? She said that she understood this but I really needed to try to make a list. Again, I cried for days and then I attempted to make the list but without success. It seemed to me that I was reducing Colin to little more than an odd job man.

My nephew, Andrew, who had been sorting out my affairs took over, and he told me that the list just had to be completed, and that he would do it on my behalf. He sat with me and very gently and kindly made me think about the financial losses I had incurred due to Colin's untimely death. It was such a difficult exercise but somehow together we managed it and Andrew submitted it to the Solicitors. I know that these things have to be done, but it does have the effect of demeaning the memory of someone who is dearly loved. Shortly after this the offer was upped to £12,000.

The second very traumatic event was when I was contacted by Jonathan who told me that the hospital wanted written permission to obtain Colin's records from the GP. I told him that I had no problem with this, and he said he would send me the form to sign for their release. He then told me that Walsgrave Hospital also wanted me to sign a written consent form to release my medical records and my Personnel records from work!!! I was incandescent with rage as I could not understand how they dare intrude on my privacy. It just seemed like one more outrage that Walsgrave could perpetrate against me. Yes, Colin had died needlessly in their care, and I could understand the request for his records, but how dare they ask for mine. I told Jonathan that under no circumstances would they have my records and that I felt this was an infringement of my privacy and an outrage. He said he would relay this information to them. I telephoned my Personnel Officer at work and told him about the request and that they were not to be given access to my records. He was as outraged as me at the request and assured me that the records would not be released. I could not believe the sheer audacity of the hospital's Legal Department which felt that it was acceptable to start hounding me for my records! Had they not done enough to me. I felt victimised. Jonathan advised them that I would not release my records and they said they would go to Court. I told them I would be quite prepared to appear before a Judge and state my case. At this point I was offered £20,000.

I felt that my mental state was deteriorating. I was tearful all the time and felt so unhappy. A meeting was arranged in Birmingham to discuss the situation face to face with Jonathan and his colleague, and Andrew came with me. Jonathan explained that going to Court would not be easy and that a Judge could, if he chose, insist that my records be released anyway. He also reminded me that I had always maintained that the case was not motivated by monetary gain and that the hospital had now admitted liability. He advised that I carefully consider the offer before me. Andrew advised that I should now accept the offer because he was concerned about the impact all this was having on my physical and mental health.

I knew they were all right but a small vengeful part of me wanted to continue, not because I wanted more money but because I wanted to make their lives as difficult as I could. I did agree to accept the offer but on condition that I got a full and frank apology, and that systems were put in place to reduce the risk of this happening to someone else.

When Andrew and I left Jonathan's office we walked into Birmingham City Centre and talked things through. He was very honest and told me he did not recognise the person I had become, and the impact of all of this was changing my personality. He said he was so pleased that I had accepted the offer, and said he now wanted me to try to move on with my life. We looked in the jewellers and he said that he felt I should buy something with some of the money. He wanted me to buy a ring and wear it proudly. He said he knew Colin would love that. I did not do it that day but I did later along the line. I reflected on what Andrew had said to me that day and I knew it was true, and I resolved to return to the person Colin had fallen in love with. I knew this would not be easy, life events have a profound effect and do definitely change you but I knew that is what Colin would want.

A few days later Jonathan phoned me and asked me if I wanted to go public about the offer and involve the Media. It took me a nano second to make that decision. Here was the opportunity to tell the world at large what had happened to Colin in Walsgrave Hospital and that the Trust was now admitting liability. The story made the local and national newspapers and local television news on both channels. I had to be interviewed as did Jonathan who was his usual supportive self. It was so sad to see Colin's smiling face looking out at me from newspapers and television screens, but I knew he would feel that "justice had prevailed".
After the interviews Jonathan gave me a hug and told me that Colin would be proud of me and the work I had done,

and because I had so much respect for him that meant so much to me.

At this point I felt that there was little more that could be done and that now was the time to let go and try to move on. Of course, Colin would be with me forever, no matter what I did or where I went. He is the last thing I think about every night and the first thing I think about every morning. I had to do some things with my life to make it more meaningful. I carried on working as an agency social worker. The family bought an apartment in Portugal and I managed the sale and getting it set up and furnished. I spent time there, but I missed Colin so much. I just felt somehow the hospital had got off very lightly. However, I accepted I just had to let it go and move on with my life.

CHAPTER 12
AIRING THE ISSUES

Then one day out of the blue I received a telephone call from a Sky News researcher. She asked me how I felt about the new super hospital which was about to open on the Walsgrave site. I told her that in my view you could have all the super state of the art hospitals in the world but if you moved the same culture, the same staff with the same attitudes into the building nothing would ever change. My view is that it is people not buildings that make hospitals successful. She then told me that there was going to be a live programme from Walsgrave fronted by Adam Boulton, the Political Editor of Sky News, and that someone extremely important would be taking part. She said she was unable to tell me who it was because of security requirements but that it was about as important as you could get. I realised then that it was probably Tony Blair, the then Prime Minister. She then asked me if I would like to take part and put a question to the "important guest". I said I would be delighted to do so. I then had to tell her who would be coming with me so they could be cleared by security. I decided that my friend Gill should come as she would stop me getting emotional. The researcher also told me that a television crew would come to my home and interview me before the live show, which they did.

On the morning of the programme I arrived at the hospital with Gill and we were given our seats. It was quite nerve-racking knowing that the programme was going out live on national television and that Sky TV is broadcast throughout Europe but I saw it as another opportunity. For the Trust this was quite a coup having the Prime Minister visit their new super hospital and they were going to make the most of it. We saw the Chief Executive glance in our direction and when he saw me sitting there he did a double-take, and it was obvious he saw me as a fly in the ointment of his success. In spite of the nerves, both Gill and I had a little giggle.

The show progressed and when it was my turn to speak Adam Boulton told the audience what had happened to Colin and asked me to put a question to Tony Blair. I told him that when someone dies in such circumstances the family usually does not want to go to litigation, it just wants answers.

However it is forced to litigate to get those answers because there is no honesty or transparency in the system. I pointed out that this is a huge waste of public funds which could be used for patient care. I asked him what action he intended to take to ensure that when mistakes happen they are dealt with in an open, honest and safe way. Tony Blair waffled on as is his wont. He said that he could not comment on individual cases and he felt sure that any words he could say to me would be of little comfort. He then went on to tell me that if I felt that I had been treated badly, there were processes in place for dealing with this! He continued saying that plans were in place to deal with salaries and that the likely outcome was that this would improve services. To say I was underwhelmed by his response is a gross understatement, he had totally side-stepped the question. His answer just confirmed that he had no idea about what was happening in hospitals on the ground and no will to put things right.

However, I told myself that the answer was not as important as publicising the issue and I felt pleased that I had done that much at least. Following on from my questioning, another member of the audience tried to bring him back to the subject but without success.

Several other people had put questions to the Prime Minister when a member of staff from the hospital raised his hand and said he wished to speak to me. He then said publicly that if I wished to telephone him after the show he would be happy to answer any questions I had. I responded by telling him that his offer was gratifying but that it had taken three years and national television before it had been forthcoming. I did not take up his offer; I was finished with Walsgrave Hospital.

As Gill and I left the auditorium where the programme had taken place I was approached by a reporter from a Birmingham Newspaper for an interview. I began talking to her when we were approached by two members of hospital security. One of the gentlemen told me that I could not give an interview in the building. This was in spite of the fact that several other people who had put questions to the Prime Minister were being interviewed without interference. I responded by saying OK and that we would go outside. We continued the interview outside; when again security approached and said the interview could not take place on hospital land. I thought they were joking and laughed. I pointed out that we were in the car park. He persisted in asking us to move off the hospital site. Gill was insistent we stay put and said that they should phone the police if they felt that was appropriate and I now know she was so right, but at the time I felt it was more important for me to continue to maintain my dignity as I had done throughout the whole trauma of Colin's death, and wished to do so now. Before leaving the site we asked security from where the direction to move us had emanated and they said it came directly from hospital management. We decided to leave without making a fuss but the hilarious thing was that at the time I was working in the hospital and so whilst security saw us off the site, I walked around the block and back into the hospital to my office.

I had promised to phone Jonathan after the show to give him an update and I told him about what had happened. We had a good laugh as he said that my street cred had gone up a few notches as even he had not been ordered off the hospital site.

The following day I went to the crematorium with some flowers for Colin and I just knew he would have been really proud with the action we had all taken and that he would have been so amused by the fact that his story got as far as the Prime Minister. This also had the effect of enabling me to move on a little because I felt that I had achieved what I had set out to do.

CHAPTER 13
CONCLUSION

It is now nearly twelve years since Colin's untimely and tragic death and whilst much has changed in the world, there still appear to be "accidents" happening in hospitals nationwide, resulting in the loss of much loved people. We regularly hear that, "lessons have been learned," but have they? I think not.

In the years following Colin's death I have been approached for help and guidance by three different families who have lost loved ones in similar situations to that experienced by Colin in the same hospital. I have also read extensively about the situation within Stafford Hospital and seen eleven hospitals placed into "special measures". Statistics show that last year alone 3,500 people died unnecessarily in NHS hospitals and these were the deaths that were reported. The causes of these deaths included patients being given the wrong medicine, fatal surgical mistakes and staff failing to spot patients' deteriorating conditions.

I have had both time and reason to reflect on the problems within NHS hospitals and what some of the issues are.
I believe wholeheartedly in the NHS but I also believe it has lost sight of some fundamental and important issues. Managers do not appreciate the fact that the most important person in the hospital is the patient! Not the Chief Executive, not the Chair of the Trust, not the arrogant, learned consultant or the Ward Manager, but the patient. That is its raison d'être but this ethos seems to have long since been forgotten. Somewhere along the way priorities seem to have changed and targets and managers take preference over patients. It is a great irony that in a person centred profession, the person is not always considered as important as other players. If the patient is put first and genuinely listened too, mistakes will decrease.

If the families of patients are listened to, rather than being seen as an annoying interruption to life on the ward, perhaps accidents would be avoided.

Certain language is used within hospitals which is worrying. A couple of examples illustrate this clearly, when statistics were being discussed about the number of people being admitted/discharged to and from hospital I heard them referred to as, "throughput." I am sure that we have all heard the phrase, "bed blockers," used when referring to elderly people who cannot be discharged due to other than medical reasons. Why not just use the words, "people or person," because that's what they are – not statistics but some-one's loved one. Using appropriate language ensures that this is kept in mind.

I feel that on some wards nursing has lost its way. I do appreciate that some nurses work extremely hard and that many wards are short staffed and the pressure on nurses can be high. However, some attitudes need to change. In Colin's case it was obvious from the Inquest that the nurses' notes were inaccurate and done retrospectively and if he had been cared for as he should have been, it would have been plainly obvious to nursing staff that the man was really sick. We hear on a daily basis that old people who are unable to feed themselves sometimes go hungry and thirsty, or are left in their own excrement, as there is no response to the nurses call bell, something I witnessed myself when I was admitted to hospital. I find it hard to understand why a group of nurses is often seen at the nursing station, giggling and chatting when they could be interacting with patients and observing their condition. If there is time to spare it should be spent with patients, not socialising with colleagues. This is so important because doctors visit for a few minutes on ward rounds, whilst nurses have patients in their care for a whole shift. It is their responsibility to observe effectively and diligently pass information to the doctors. If this had happened in Colin's case the outcome might have been very different.

Because of their hierarchical nature, a culture exists within some hospitals which is bullying and which produces a climate of fear among staff, particularly those who are in junior positions. This atmosphere makes it difficult if not impossible for staff to ask for help or to openly admit that they have made a mistake. This culture ensures that openness and transparency are often strangers within a hospital environment.

When mistakes are made, from my experience, there appears to be the attitude that these are not admitted at any cost. If a complaint is made some hospitals immediately go on the defensive rather than seeing a complaint as an opportunity to improve. If real lessons are to be learned listening to and analysing a complaint are positive and constructive ways to improve systems. This is so important as many "medical accidents" come about as a result of systemic failures.

Because of the lack of openness and the closing of ranks, families often have to resort to seeking legal advice. I truly believe that most do not want to do this but they desperately need answers which are not forthcoming. This is a sad state of affairs for all concerned, not least the British tax payer who picks up the tab, and it is an enormous tab. The cost to the NHS for the year 2011/12 was £1.2 billion which represented compensation and legal costs and the 2013/2014 NHS budget has set aside £22.7 billion to cover medical negligence liabilities. It almost seems as though they are planning to fail!

I know that in my own case, I used my household insurance which had legal cover up to £50,000 and in my naivety I assumed that this would more than cover the case. However, it was not long before that money had run out, and the legal firm provided the rest on a "no win no fee basis". Of course, I was pleased that they did because without them I could not have continued but in effect this escalated the costs to the NHS. When the case came to a conclusion I received £20,000 compensation but the legal costs must have been well in excess of £100,000. The net result is that there are some very successful and wealthy law firms operating. I am not criticising them. I only have praise for Jonathan Peacock, the solicitor who represented me. However, what I do have issue with is a NHS Trust which will defend an indefensible claim, racking up legal costs at a monumental rate at the tax payers expense thereby depriving the NHS of funds which could have been spent on patient care. My case is replicated on a daily basis throughout the country and one can only imagine the sums involved, and this is at the same time when newspapers regularly publish stories about cancer patients who are denied life prolonging drugs because of the cost. It just does not make economic sense to squander NHS funds on litigation. Some of these cases need never have gone to litigation if Trusts held their hands up to their failings, learned to say, "We Are sorry," genuinely learned from their mistakes and were honest about what these lessons were and what measures would be put in place to ensure their mistakes are not repeated.

Of course, it is not just the amounts paid out in legal expenses and compensation which are outrageous, but the time staff expend on preparing for Inquests, GMC enquiries and other enquiries which are often pursued. In Colin's case, I am sure that had we been dealt with differently at the time of his death in a caring, open, honest and transparent manner, we would not have felt the need to go to Inquest, the General Medical Council and to litigation and if we are a typical family which I believe we are, it is not difficult to imagine the hours that could be saved and the pain which could be avoided because the human costs far outweigh the financial ones.

Perhaps it is time for the Government to consider instituting a system similar to the Criminal Injuries Compensation Scheme, where set amounts are laid down and paid to victims.

Whilst such a scheme would have its difficulties, at least there would not be years of wrangling and prolonged legal battles to be endured while the cash registers are working overtime.

I have asked myself what lessons I have learned from the whole experience and there are many. The first thing I would say is that if your loved one is in the hospital and does not appear to be improving despite doctors protestations that they are, follow your instincts. You know that person better than anyone, and if you are not happy with their progress, insist on seeing another doctor, preferably a Consultant and express your concerns. If the doctors are planning a discharge from hospital and you are sure that this is inappropriate again follow your instincts, and challenge the decision. Remember that doctors are human, and humans make mistakes. Ask yourself, what's the worst that can happen? They might get annoyed – tough! How I wish I had had this advice. I might not be writing this book now.

If after discharge you are not happy with the condition of your loved one, even though you have been told it will take some time before things improve, follow your instincts. Obviously post surgery people are unwell but if you believe recovery is not taking the normal path, get them back into hospital. Do not procrastinate or be concerned that you are over-reacting if your instincts are telling you all is not well, it probably is not. Even if you get it wrong, does it really matter?

If your loved one dies and you feel that something was amiss, it probably was. Do not collect the death certificate but instead phone the Coroner's office to discuss the death.

Remember, you only get one chance. Once you have buried or cremated the person, you have buried or cremated the mistakes.

Ask the hospital for answers and put everything in writing so that you have a paper trail and evidence. Ask for a meeting with the Chief Executive and the Consultant involved but be sure to take some-one with you. At this point hopefully you may get the answers you need which may help you move forward. If however, you do not, you might decide that you need to take some further action. Always ensure that any lawyer you consult is an expert in medical negligence cases.

If this is the route you decide to go down I would say, "Be prepared." It is a long, winding, and painful road on which many obstacles are encountered. You are challenging a huge bureaucratic machine which has the potential to crush individuals. You will need to be determined and courageous to take on that machine but you can do it because you have right on your side and the outcome will be the answers you are dying for, for you and your loved one.

Printed in Great Britain
by Amazon